GW00569971

AIRSPEED

AIRSPEED

The company and its aeroplanes

by

D. H. MIDDLETON

TERENCE DALTON LIMITED
LAVENHAM . SUFFOLK

1982

Published by
TERENCE DALTON LIMITED

ISBN 0 86138 009 6

Text photoset in 11/12pt. Garamond

Printed in Great`Britain at
The Lavenham Press Limited, Lavenham, Suffolk
© D. H. Middleton 1982

Contents

Introduction

THE idea of writing this book came to me in 1967 after reading Martin Sharp's excellent history of de Havilland. I recalled the many fascinating hours I had spent in recent years with Hessell and Miriam Tiltman, with whom I had become friendly through a chance business matter, listening to many stories of the early days of Airspeed which he formed with Nevil Shute Norway, whose greater fame in the literary world under his nom-de-plume Nevil Shute in no way diminishes his achievement in aviation.

I was surprised and disappointed by the scant credit given to Airspeed by Sharp whose company, de Havilland, had taken them over in 1940. I resolved, in spite of having no experience in authorship, to record the history of Airspeed before all the original members of the company had passed on. Even if the manuscript only reposed in the archives of the Royal Aeronautical Society, I felt it to be worth the effort.

Many visits to ex-Airspeed men, from directors to fitters, armed with a tape-recorder produced about ten hours of reminiscences which confirmed the tremendous spirit I recalled from my year at Airspeed in 1938 before moving on to the de Havilland Technical School.

Having written two chapters, I learned that H. A. Taylor was writing for Putnam his very comprehensive book on Airspeed aircraft. I placed all my data at Tony Taylor's disposal and did no more work until 1974 when Richard Riding, the Editor of *Aeroplane Monthly*, asked me to write the first of a series of articles in his journal covering a number of Airspeed types. This revived my interest in the original project, which was to be an attempt to re-create the atmosphere of the exciting pre-war years of a fascinating industry when it was being built by individualists prepared to gamble their all, including their lives, on their hunches and their confidence in their own ability. No vast corporations with huge teams of anonymous computerised technicians spending tens of millions of pounds on the tail or fuselage of an international design, just a few people sweating blood and having fun, for fun it certainly was for much of the time, and it was their money that was being spent.

So this book is dedicated to those people, the Tiltmans, Norways, Cobhams and Grimthorpes, who built this marvellous industry, and to their wives who had some of the fun and a lot of the worry.

I am indebted to many people, and the ladies must be at the top of the list. Mrs Miriam Tiltman, who thought of the name "Airspeed" and, with her late husband, Hessell, entertained me so many times with hours of reminiscence; Mrs G. B. S. Errington, who kindly gave me access to her husband's papers; Mrs Sheila Darby; Mrs Valerie Colman, whose late husband was Airspeed's first test pilot; Mrs Dorothy Clanchy, who spent many hours in the Library of the Royal Aeronautical Society extracting information (thanks also to Mr Naylor, the Librarian, for permitting her to do so) and my wife, who commendably, and with good grace, accepted that the book must take precedence over many domestic jobs!

I am grateful to Richard Riding, Editor of *Aeroplane Monthly*, for permission to reproduce text and photographs which had already appeared in that journal. Tony Taylor's book *Airspeed Aircraft since 1931* was an invaluable source of data for cross-checking purposes. Messrs A. F. Watt, Nevil

Hessell Tiltman and Mrs Miriam Tiltman.

Shute's agent, kindly permitted me to quote from *Slide Rule*. My thanks are due to the Editors of the Royal Australian and South African Air Force Journals.

The Ministry of Defence (Air), The Imperial War Museum, The Royal Air Force Museum, The Royal Aircraft Establishment and British Airways have given valuable assistance, whilst Brigadier George Chatterton D.S.O., O.B.E., and Mr Leslie Udall told many stories of Horsa operations. Captain R. E. Gillman, D.F.C., D.F.M. contributed stories of the Ambassador in service with B.E.A., Mr Frank Horridge of Dan-Air gave useful data on the Ambassador in Dan-Air service. Captain J. H. Orrell, O.B.E., and Mr W. J. Clennell, late of the Aeronautical Inspection Directorate, were a source of valuable information whilst the ex-Airspeed people I met were numerous. In particular I must mention Sir Alan Cobham, W. F. Shaylor, David Little, Alfred Townsley, P. E. Gordon Marshall, J. Liddell, A. E. Ellison, Ron Clear, Bob Milne, Walter Locke, R. W. Cantello, Nick Carter, R. D. King, G. Wrigley, W. C. Ffitch, John Jupp, C. Chapleo, George Briggs, D. H. Wilson, J. H. Darley, J. Barrett, J. Ainsworth, Fred Headley, D. Diamond, F. Wainwright, R. Durkin, R. Palmer, F. G. Boreham, Arthur Bowen, and George Statham.

A line-up of Oxford Mk. Is at R.A.F. South Cerney, Gloucestershire, in 1938. The Oxford was probably the best known and certainly the most successful of the aircraft built by Airspeed up to the time of its takeover by de Havilland.   *Aeroplane Monthly*

George Twyman told many entertaining stories, Concord and Cavendish Morton, who were the artists responsible for Airspeed publicity, were most helpful, as were Brian Mead of the *Christchurch Times*, Capt. H. A. M. Pascoe, A.F.C., C. F. Parker, J. J. Parkes of Alvis Ltd who filled in the details of the Rapier Courier, as did Air Vice Marshal Amyas Borton, Basil Clarke contributed the report on airborne television. E. Chris Wren kindly permitted me to use his cartoons and verse and Air Vice Marshal A. G. Dudgeon provided details of the Iraqi raid on Habbaniya. I am also grateful to J. Farquharson-Robertson, archivist at Flight Refuelling Ltd., and Fred Slingsby of Kirbymoorside.

I am particularly indebted to the Marquess of Zetland for his interest and his generous foreword, and to my friend Lou Warwick for reading the manuscript and making most valuable suggestions.

In the interest of clarity the chronology of the book is aircraft type orientated, the story of each machine being continued to its end.

D. H. MIDDLETON.

Foreword

by
The Marquess of Zetland
(Formerly Lord Ronaldshay)

THE author has suggested that, as I must be the only senior Airspeed executive left now, I should write a foreword to his book. This I am delighted to do, but not as a past senior executive, for I never reached that exalted rank!

I joined Airspeed in its early days through the good offices of my uncle, Lord Grimthorpe, with little or no knowledge of the business, but as the proud holder of a pilots 'A' Licence and with the willingness to do anything I could in the field of aviation. Indeed everyone connected with the company, including the expert designers N. S. Norway and Hessell Tiltman, were willing to turn their hands to anything in those days. In fact, my earliest recollection of Airspeed Limited was of a company with a wonderful spirit, tremendous enthusiasm and a great sense of purpose.

I, myself, was soon to leave the parent company to form a new one, R. K. Dundas Limited, in conjunction with my great friend Ronald King, who was to remain with Airspeed for some time to come before also moving to R. K. Dundas Limited with the object of acting as agents for Airspeed Limited in India. It was in this connection that I became better acquainted with those early Airspeed products, the Ferry, Courier and Envoy, whose stories will be unfolded in this book.

I look back with considerable nostalgia upon the early exploits of Airspeed, and I well remember the thrill of the first landing of the Courier, being the first British aeroplane with a retractable undercarriage, the plans and hopes, and the nagging worries of the uncertain financial situations of a young company in a rapidly expanding industry. I also remember, of course, my first solo flight from India to this country in an Armstrong-Siddeley Cheetah V engined Courier belonging to R. K. Dundas Limited.

To me, therefore, it seems a splendid thing that Mr. Middleton is putting the Airspeed story on paper, and I hope that those who read this book will derive as much enjoyment from it as we did from taking part in the events which it describes.

CHAPTER ONE

Tern and Ferry

IN spite of one of the worst economic depressions in history the early 'Thirties saw the formation of several small aircraft companies at a time when determination and 'guesstimation' produced some first-class aeroplanes in a few months. In technical terms, one of the most successful was Airspeed Limited. Its success was, sadly, only in the technical sense, profit eluding the company for much of its life.

Airspeed Limited was an act of faith on the part of four men, Nevil Shute Norway, Alfred Hessell Tiltman, Sir Alan Cobham and Lord Grimthorpe, a Yorkshire landowner who risked large sums of money to ensure the ultimate success of the venture in which he had great faith and which rose like a phoenix from the ashes of the grandiose and ill-fated National Airship Project. Norway is now chiefly remembered for his novels under the pen name Nevil Shute. Tiltman's feeling for line and elegance, doubtless stimulated by his close association with Geoffrey de Havilland, produced some of the most graceful aeroplanes ever designed. Sir Alan Cobham's pioneer work with Airspeed led to the formation of Flight Refuelling Limited, in which Tiltman was responsible for much of the technical work.

Nevil Norway was born in London in 1899 and, as he recounts in his autobiography *Slide Rule*, had built several model aeroplanes by the time he was thirteen. After the First World War he studied engineering at Oxford. He was fortunate to meet C. C. Walker, an engineer with The Aircraft Manufacturing Company at Hendon. Walker invited Norway to join Airco, as the company was known, on a part-time basis during vacations. This gave him valuable experience on design and wind tunnel research with Walker who, in 1920, with Captain de Havilland and Frank Hearle, formed the de Havilland Aircraft Company at Stag Lane Aerodrome near London. Joining de Havilland on a full-time basis in 1923, he worked as a junior stressman and performance calculator.

Hessell Tiltman completed his education at London University and, at the age of 19, left for Canada with a B.Sc and £8 in his pocket. He joined the design staff working on the Quebec Bridge, a job which gave him a thorough training in structural design and a grandstand view of the centre span falling into the river when an hydraulic ram failed almost at the top of the lift.

Being diabetic and lame he was not fit for war service. In 1916 he entered the Airco Design Office at Hendon and flew with many famous pilots. Having

formation of Oxford Is from R.A.F. South Cerney, Gloucestershire.

The Aeroplane

1

been responsible for many of the stress calculations, and knowing only too well some of their limitations, he was often frightened. He said that vertical dives unnerved him and he often wished he had specified quarter-inch bolts instead of 2BA! In those days the only authority on stressing was a book by Professors Pippard and Pritchard called, ominously, *The Snag*. His work with de Havilland and Arthur Hagg, who many years later became technical director of Airspeed, ensured that Tiltman was continually stimulated by technical innovation.

A. Hessell Tiltman, B.Sc., F.R.Ae.S.

After the war Airco decided to attack some world speed records by converting a DH.9 biplane into a racing machine. Hessell Tiltman, responsible for performance calculations, lay along a board in the rear fuselage looking through a small window. The pilot hurtled along straight lengths of railway line just above the track whilst his observer checked the times between previously selected stations. On one double journey they attained a mean speed of 165 mph (266 km/hr) and set up a few world records. Airco had extravagant ideas for the development of international aviation; unfortunately they were premature, the world was not ready for air transport on a large scale, and Airco went into liquidation.

Tiltman joined de Havillands in 1921 and worked with many ex-Airco colleagues, including Nevil Norway. He flew regularly with Cobham, Hope and Barnard, all of whom became famous in the interwar years for their record breaking and sporting flying activities. These were carefree days in the industry, although money was very short. Among other things de Havilland bought surplus military aeroplanes for conversion into more peaceful roles.

Test flying was highly unscientific. Tiltman and Hope once found themselves descending through cloud over the North Sea as darkness fell. Though they had no compass and very little fuel left, Hope was unconcerned and, quite intuitively, safely reached an aerodrome on the Thames Estuary. During this period Tiltman flew in aircraft ranging from the DH.60 Moth to the DH.66 Hercules air liner. Pilots invariably wore a parachute; the observer was not so fortunate, presumably being considered expendable. Tiltman once asked Mr Hearle what to do in the event of an emergency; apparently there was no easy answer as the firm could not afford another parachute. He recalled slamming the door in disgust as he left the office.

In the mid-Twenties the likelihood of the aeroplane being developed for long-distance travel was hardly credible. It was decided by the Government that Britain should build two very large airships, R.100 and R.101, for the Empire Air Routes. The R.100 was to be built by private enterprise, the Airship Guarantee Company, a Vickers subsidiary, whilst R.101 was to be built by the Government Airship Establishment at Cardington. So the State and private enterprise were in direct competition.

The Airship Guarantee Company had to meet rigid performance specifications before the Government would accept their ship. The trials were to culminate in a fifty-two-hour endurance flight. In the case of R.100, shareholders' money was at stake, the incentives were firmly established. No such criteria were set for the State-built R.101. Public funds were available, so the incentives were not of the same order.

In charge of the Howden design team was Barnes Wallis, the brilliant engineer whose geodetic construction system led to the Wellesley and Wellington bombers and whose work on the Blockbuster and bouncing bombs made a considerable contribution to victory in the Second World War. In 1924 Norway joined Wallis as chief calculator, and five years later he became deputy chief engineer. By this time Hessell Tiltman had joined him. Sir Dennistoun Burney was in overall command.

R.100 was 750 feet (230m) long, 130 feet (39.2m) in diameter, and was powered by six Rolls-Royce Condor engines developing a total of 1,400 hp. When she flew in December, 1929, two months after her rival, she was greatly superior in performance and required only minor modifications. In *Slide Rule*, Norway has described in vivid terms the tragic rivalry which resulted from what he saw as jealousy on the part of the Cardington men, a rivalry which prevented them discussing with their very experienced opposite numbers at Howden the major problems which had to be faced when R.101 flew; problems which ultimately led to the destruction of the ship and the death of many of those who designed and built her.

In July, 1930, R.100 left on her proving flight to Montreal. It took 78 hours at an average speed of 42 mph (68 km/hr). The Montreal *Daily Star* of 12th August 1930, eulogised the three-hour demonstration flight over the city in purple prose which sounds most quaint today:

"The visiting craft could be seen coursing down on the city from over the mountain brow. First it hit straight for the river, and then seemed to decide that the looping (sic) might as well commence then and there. So it stuck its aerial point east and came humming down Notre Dame Street. If up to that time people seemed unaware of its approach, harbour boats, tugs and automobile sirens soon appraised the ears that the long awaited event was close at hand . . . Butcher boys and meat packers in white uniforms, grain workers with a down of wheat dust, oily garage men and a thousand other trades emerged from their work to let the sun at their tonsils while they gaped skywards. One solitary painter, a hard boiled individual who had seen everything, apparently, swung a lusty brush oblivious to sights overhead, while the boat loafed through the blue."

Apart from a minor problem of fabric ripping off the stabiliser, she behaved well all the way.

After this flight R.100 languished in her shed at Cardington to await the departure of R.101 for India. The Howden design staff worked on various schemes for the improvement of airships, including one for a ship twice the size of R.100 with even a ballroom on board. Sir Dennistoun Burney was optimistic that a new ship would be ordered in 1931.

In October Norway was told in confidence by Burney that the Airship project might be cancelled. Two days later, on 4th October R.101, totally untested after the insertion of a new hull section to give her the lifting capacity she needed, left Cardington for India. Seven and a half hours later, in appalling weather, she crashed in darkness on a hill near Beauvais in Northern France. Most of her crew and all the passengers, including Lord Thomson, the Air Minister, and Sir Sefton Brancker, the Director General of Civil Aviation, perished in the blazing wreck. Only the R.A.F. ensign flying from its staff on the tail cone escaped the flames.

The effect of this disaster on the Airship scheme was catastrophic. On 1st November all the staff of The Airship Guarantee Company were given one month's notice of the closure of the plant. R.100 was sold for scrap and broken up in her hangar at Cardington. Her wheel adorns the entrance hall at R.A.F. Cardington to this day. Norway worked very hard at this time to help the dismissed workers in finding alternative positions.

Norway and Tiltman had decided upon their course of action. They would start their own aircraft company. They had already carried out market research and decided that the private owner market would be responsive to a two/three-seater aircraft. In *Slide Rule* Norway refers to it as a monoplane, but there is little doubt that it was, in fact, a biplane for which a comprehensive and elaborate brochure was prepared.

Norway decided that the company name was of considerable importance and that it should begin with "A" so that in any aviation directory or air display programme the name should be near the top. Miriam Tiltman, Hessell's wife, suggested "AIRSPEED". It was agreed to be most appropriate and euphonious.

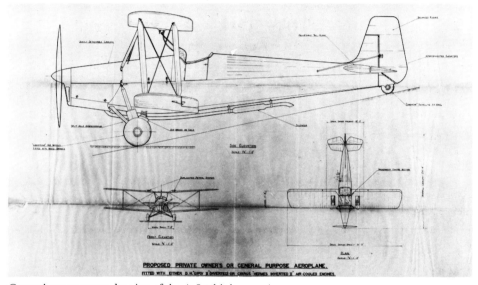

General arrangement drawing of the A.S.3 biplane project.

The two men approached possible investors. The economy of the country was in a catastrophic state and few were prepared to consider risking their money, although they showed interest.

An exception was Lord Grimthorpe, a Yorkshire landowner with his own aircraft. He invested £3,000 and was invited to become chairman of the company. In *Slide Rule* Norway paid tribute to him:

"He supported the company throughout its early difficulties to an extent which would have been a burden to the wealthiest of men. Without his support initially I do not think the company could have started; without his continuous financial support in the years that followed it would certainly have come to grief. . ."

Years later one of Lord Grimthorpe's friends told Norway of Grimthorpe's answer to the suggestion that it would be best to cut his losses and get out of such an unprofitable speculation. He replied that the business interested him and he thought it would do well in the end. The money was being spent in wages in his district of Yorkshire where unemployment was high. He felt that it was his duty to hazard his money to try to create employment; if the money was lost he would have the satisfaction of knowing that he had provided a livelihood for a number of men during the years of depression.

Sir Alan Cobham was one of the first people to be approached. Cobham knew Norway and Tiltman well from the de Havilland days and had himself become famous for his pioneering and record-breaking flights all over the world. He had served in the Royal Flying Corps and, after demobilisation, carried 5,000 passengers in a flying tour of Britain. In 1921 he joined de Havilland to start the DH. Hire Service. From two aircraft and one pilot he developed it to fifteen aircraft and twelve pilots. Cobham carried out many pioneering flights including, in 1923, a 12,000-mile (19,000 km) flight through Europe, North Africa, Egypt and Palestine. In 1924 he won the King's Cup Race and flew from England to Rangoon and back; in 1925 he flew from London to Capetown with Sir Sefton Brancker on a survey flight. In 1926 he went to Australia and back in a DH.50 single-engine biplane and commanded a Short Singapore flying boat on a 23,000 mile (37,000 km) survey flight around the African continent.

Sir Alan won the Britannia Trophy in 1923 and 1925, and, among other honours, was awarded the Royal Aero Club Gold Medal in 1925. This was the calibre of the man who was to give his support to Airspeed, a man whose work with them ultimately led to the formation of his own Flight Refuelling Limited, world leaders in the technique of airborne refuelling of high-speed aircraft.

The bus garage in York in which Airspeed Limited was formed, photographed by the author in 1968.

Norway and Tiltman decided that the interior of the proposed biplane must have a finish equal to that of a good motor-car and the safety of the occupants would be greatly enhanced if the side-by-side seats were in a cockpit as far aft as possible so that, in the event of a crash, a substantial length of fuselage would absorb the impact before the occupants hit the ground. This exercise in "crashworthiness" was rather spoiled by the idea of having the third seat forward of the cockpit, although normally the space would be used for luggage. The design was very versatile, with many variants.

The G.A. drawing reveals a very handsome aircraft powered by a Gipsy III or Cirrus Hermes II inverted engine. A span of 31 feet (9.48m) reduced to 10 feet (3.06m) with wings folded. The overall length was 24 feet 4 inches (7.46m) and the wheel track 7 feet (2.14m). Great stress was laid upon ease of taxiing and the hazards of slavishly following the current trend of low wing loading and low landing speed which made most aeroplanes very vulnerable to gusts near the ground and during the taxiing run.

Despite the immense effort put into this attractive design, it was soon clear that the likelihood of raising the £20,000-£40,000 needed to start production was extremely remote.

In parallel with the drawing office activities, Norway was deeply involved in the intricacies of preparing a Prospectus and forming the new company. A. E. Hewitt, a leading York solicitor, well known to Norway, took a keen interest and steered him around the legal obstacles. His brother-in-law, Group Captain Baldwin, R.A.F., was invited to cast a professional eye over the project. He commented most favourably.

A search for premises in York was extremely unrewarding and Tiltman was most contemptuous, in his diary, of the local estate agents: "None of them was the slightest help . . . they did not seem to be able even to grasp what we wanted; as a matter of fact our requirements were very simple and straight-forward . . . they seemed to be a very incompetent body of people." Ultimately they discovered that the municipal bus garage was for sale, although it was larger than they required. The Town Clerk was persuaded to put before the City Council the proposition that the garage should be let for the purpose of building aeroplanes and introducing more business into the city.

On 3rd January 1931, the Prospectus draft was approved and thirty copies sent to various parties who had shown interest in supporting the firm. Tiltman thought it a weak document as the only name of significance on the new Board was Lord Grimthorpe. At best it prepared the ground, and certainly helped in strengthening the Board.

It referred to the intended manufacture of the biplane, stating that "The country stands upon the eve of a boom in aviation . . . and the manufacture of small aircraft is entering upon an era of sound business and profit." It was estimated that a production of 150 machines per year could be achieved on a capital of £40,000, representing a turnover of £112,000. It concluded, after summarising the careers of Norway and Tiltman, "As the remuneration of the Managing Director and Technical Director will depend mainly upon a percentage of the profits, the earning of profits will receive their concentrated attention."

Such resolve and profound sentiment fell upon relatively stony ground. Even at this late stage Sir Alan Cobham had not made up his mind to join them. They were in constant touch with him, writing and telephoning. He always seemed keen, and never suggested turning the proposition down. The York solicitor, Hewitt, and Group Capt. Baldwin, were also seriously contemplating an investment. Tiltman realised that, somehow, this impasse must be broken or the project must fail. At the end of January, Norway asked Hewitt if he was prepared to join the Board as Baldwin's nominee. He agreed to do so. Hewitt then had a meeting with Cobham, and, in spite of much persuasion Cobham was still unwilling to give a decision. He finally promised to meet Tiltman and Norway at his London office at 9.30 on the following Saturday morning. At 9 o'clock Cobham rang Tiltman at their hotel to ask for the meeting to be postponed for one hour. Much worse, he said that he had decided not to join the company. This was a shattering blow, but they decided to hold the meeting and try to convince him that he should change his mind. After two hours they achieved success and returned to York feeling that they had done a good day's work, as Cobham would now be a director.

At an informal Board meeting in London during the following week, at which both Cobham and Hewitt were present, the Prospectus was amended, Cobham agreeing to seek further capital and approach the Air Ministry to see if they would place an order with the company. Hessell Tiltman's diary recorded: "A fellow called T. E. Laing has been in touch with us for some time; he is a pilot who had a bad crash in the States; his ankle was smashed, but is now mending gradually and he is anxious to get back into aeronautics in England. He is willing to put £1,000 into our venture and wants a job. He is willing to start in quite a modest way and appears to be quite a useful chap."

So Tom Laing became Airspeed's first employee. He was a remarkable character with great enthusiasm and drive. University educated, he served an apprenticeship at Metropolitan Vickers and inherited £10,000. In the First World War he flew Bristol Fighters and was demobbed with the rank of captain. After a period fruit farming with his brother in Canada, he ran a speedboat ferry service on one of the lakes. This quickly reduced him to penury.

He rode the buffers of a freight train to the U.S.A. to find work, took charge of a platelaying gang on the Santa Fe Railroad for two years and then returned to aviation as pilot of a Curtiss Jenny joyriding machine. During the winter he worked at the Ford Aircraft factory at Detroit. He next became a flying instructor, but a pupil crashed the aircraft and Laing suffered a badly crushed foot which caused him to walk heavily with a stick for the rest of his life. He served Airspeed well until his death in a car crash at the beginning of Second World War. His commencing salary at York was £300 per year.

Frustrations abounded, there were many people who appeared to be most enthusiastic about the company and would probably invest in it. Morale boosting meetings mostly came to naught. The time and mental energy wasted was immense and the strain on Norway and Tiltman was considerable. The discussions with the city council over the bus garage seemed interminable. Not until the Board Meeting of 20th February was the company able to make decisions.

Cobham maintained that 1931 would see a boom in gliding and that there would be a good market for a high-performance aircraft which could be

The A.S.1 Tern sailplane — a 1/48th scale model made by the author.

launched by towing behind a car. It was decided that a design should be commenced immediately as it was relatively inexpensive to build and would turn money over while the powered aeroplane was being developed. The Prospectus was amended accordingly to include a reference to this project. Tiltman moved into a room in York which served as a drawing office where the General Arrangement drawing of the new glider was quickly completed; it looked a very sound design with a number of detail innovations which would attract gliding club members.

The Yorkshire press announced the formation of the new company on 4th March and on 7th March Norway married Dr Frances Heaton, house physician at York County Hospital. He left for a honeymoon in Switzerland taking with him data from which he was to calculate the wing section ordinates for the glider.

On 13th March 1931 Airspeed Limited was registered as a public company with a nominal capital of £50,000 in £1 shares, and 250 copies of the prospectus were issued to potential investors, including the secretaries of all the flying clubs in the country. The negotiations for the bus garage dragged on, but some progress had been made.

The response to the circulation of the Prospectus was pitiful and the extreme difficulty in obtaining risk capital became even clearer. Both men were unknown outside the aircraft industry, the economy of the country was deteriorating, so the number of potential investors in such a venture was very small indeed.

There were endless disappointments at this critical time; almost every appeal for support met with a rebuff or a half-hearted hint that something might be done later, though Amy Johnson, the famous solo flyer, invested £100.

By the middle of April Tiltman finished the G.A. drawing of the biplane, to be numbered A.S.3. The *News Chronicle* announced the formation of Airspeed Limited, stating that "The company's first venture will be the manufacture of a new type of light aeroplane, the nearest thing to a motor car on wings that has yet been evolved. Its cockpit will closely resemble the saloon interior of a luxurious little two-seater with drop windows and a sliding roof . . . " This article continued with a detailed description of the machine and its design philosophy.

Tiltman and Norway were flattered to receive a telegram of good wishes from Capt. Geoffrey de Havilland.

At a Board Meeting in April Sir Alan Cobham outlined a scheme which was to be the salvation of the company. He suggested that Airspeed should build for him two or three aircraft with seats for nine or ten passengers, a medium performance and very safe, easy to build and maintain. With these aeroplanes he planned to tour Great Britain combining publicity and propaganda with what seemed to be a profitable business. He was planning his famous National Aviation Day Displays, one of the most remarkable aviation ventures of the pre-war period. With a fleet of passenger aircraft, large and small, he toured the UK and South Africa, flying out of airports and small fields with hardly an injury to the many thousands of passengers who enjoyed the thrill of flying for the first time.

Airspeed's financial position was dealt a severe blow when a promise of support by an industrial group in York was withdrawn. The minimum target figure was now completely out of reach. Sir Alan tried vainly to interest the Napier Aero Engine Company, and, on the day the issue closed, 25th April, a total of £5,300 had been subscribed. This ruled out any possibility of building the powered aircraft, so Norway suggested that the only solution was to adopt Cobham's original suggestion to build the glider and take whatever consultancy work was available. The A.S.3 project was abandoned. Hessell Tiltman had, however, completed a G.A. drawing of a twin DH. Gipsy-engined biplane for Cobham. It would carry eleven passengers.

In May the legal formalities necessary to reduce the authorised working capital of the company were completed. Sanction to commence trading was received from the Registrar of Companies. This event was marred by an unfortunate contretemps with the bank, whose manager had given consent to the use of its name on the Airspeed letter heading. A demand was received from this gentleman for a fee of 100 guineas for the privilege. The Airspeed Board was furious and approached the manager of another bank who waived all such claims. The account was immediately transferred.

The design of Cobham's aircraft was altered to take a third engine and Tiltman began to realise that he could not handle the design work alone. He approached A. E. Ellison, a fine engineer with whom he had worked since the de Havilland days. To his delight Ellison agreed to join Airspeed.

After a final battle with the Corporation, occupation of the bus garage was negotiated as a joint tenancy with the Universal Tyre Company. Immediate action was taken to commence production of the glider. The weak finances made it imperative that an initial batch of three should be built as quickly as possible. During the Depression it was not difficult to recruit staff. Tiltman had a draughtsman in his office whilst Norway and Tom Laing, the Works Manager, controlled seven woodworkers.

As it was not possible to move into the bus garage immediately, small premises were rented locally so that men could commence work on simple components such as wing and tailplane ribs. As soon as they were able to move into the garage Norway and Laing, sharing an office eight feet (2.4m) square, quickly installed the simple machinery and benches for the woodworkers. The aircraft was called the A.S.1. Tern and assembly of the prototype began.

In the middle of July, Cobham placed a firm order for two large aeroplanes for the National Aviation Day displays. Tiltman and his small staff, in their fifteen shillings (75p) per week drawing office, continued with the detail design of the airliner whilst assembly of the Tern prototype began at the factory. It was, in its day, a high-performance sailplane and one of the best of the new generation, in which the Germans led the field. The Versailles Treaty at the end of the First World War had prohibited Germany from building powered aircraft, so all aeronautical research was directed toward motorless flight. A distance record of 150 miles (241 km) non-stop had already been set up.

Tern was designed primarily for hillside soaring, relying upon the rising air currents deflected off slopes against which the wind blew.

The structure was of spruce, with ply and fabric covering. The 50 feet (15.2m) span cantilever wing had a five-foot (1.5m) span centre section to which the extension planes were attached by an ingenious system of tapering, self-centering high tensile bolts and self-connecting aileron controls which Tilman devised to ensure rapid assembly in the field. The ex-works price was fixed at £248, rather high for the period, but inevitable if the company was to prosper.

Early in August 1931, Tern was ready for flight test. Norway had learned to fly at Stag Lane in his de Havilland days and still held his licence. A few months earlier he had taken his gliding 'A' at Sherburn in Elmet, the nearest aerodrome to York, as he intended to carry out the test flights himself. A trailer was built and for £25 a large Buick car bought. To cut down the overheads four of the eight in-line pistons were disconnected; performance suffered considerably but this was of little significance.

The aircraft was assembled at Sherburn and, with Norway at the controls, was towed into the air by the Buick. He was delighted; it flew well and was very stable. It was vitally important to obtain publicity by making record-breaking flights as quickly as possible. Neither Norway nor Laing was familiar with sailplane flying, with its dependence upon rising currents of air, so a pilot with these skills had to be recruited.

A young German, Carli Magesuppe, was in England with a friend. Both were experienced sailplane pilots and had taken flying jobs wherever they could in an attempt to leave Germany; prejudice against Germans was strong in many European countries so, as a last resort, they came to England hoping that their flying skill would enable them to stay. Norway heard of them and they came to York. Airspeed could only offer Magesuppe a pittance to fly the Tern but the publicity, if records were broken, would help his cause. So Magesuppe took over the Tern.

His method of checking structural strength intrigued Norway. He would station two men at the wing tips and, as they jerked the wing up and down, would time the natural frequency with a stopwatch. He was a very competent pilot and expressed the opinion that the Tern was the most comfortable sailplane he had flown.

Some difficulty was experienced in finding a suitable site for the record attempts. Flights were made at Ravenscar, Sutton Bank and, later, from Ingleby Greenhow in the Cleveland Hills. The British long-distance record was set up on 24th August when Magesuppe flew from Stoupe Brow to Ravenscar and Scarborough, a distance of 15 miles (24 km) in 38 minutes. The *Yorkshire Herald* reported: "Herr Magesuppe, the German gliding ace, flew from Ravenscar to Scarborough in a new type of British sailplane manufactured by Airspeed Ltd., York. . . . The feat constitutes a record for a British made sailplane. Over 1,000 visitors assembled on the sea front at Scarborough witnessed a thrilling sight when the sailplane, coming from the direction of the North Bay, passed over Gibson's boarding house into the town, turned further North, flew over the Floral Hall in the Alexandra Gardens and, from there, made a perfect descent and landing on the North Beach."

Whilst the name of Airspeed was being publicised at various flying displays, interest in the new company was created locally and investors continually sought. Some enthusiasts put small sums into it and took jobs in the works as part of their contribution. Tiltman, working under extreme pressure, produced the detail drawings of Cobham's airliner, now known as the A.S.4. Ferry. In spite of its urgency and all the associated problems, every drawing was a work of art, lined and lettered with consummate skill. Not the least of his burdens was a stressman, who, poor fellow, suffered from St. Vitus's Dance. The distractions were too much for Tiltman, who had to ask him to find another job.

The financial situation was a continual worry. Purchasing was a primitive art; if a worker wanted tools or materials he would visit the local supplier, pay

A Ferry under construction at York. A Tern fuselage can be seen suspended from the roof.

Airspeed Limited

13

A Ferry flying over Portsmouth aerodrome.

The News, Portsmouth

cash and draw the money, if there was any, when he returned to the works. It was not uncommon for men to come in on a Friday to be told "Sorry lads, there is nobody here to get any money out of the bank, you must wait until we can contact someone with authority. You'll be in on Saturday, won't you? We can get you about two pounds and you can have some more on Monday."

A contemporary letter of appointment offered a fitter "Straight time at 1/6½ (7½p) per hour. When working on bonus, base time at 1/4 (6½p) per hour, bonus at 1/1 (5½p) per hour. Overtime at time and a quarter for the first two hours, time and a half for the remainder."

In October 1931, Tern was entered for a gliding contest near Brighton. The pilots were Carli Magesuppe and Major H. Petre, husband of Mrs Kay Petre, the well-known Brooklands racing driver. Major Petre flew Tern into second place in the Distance Competition for the de Havilland Cup and won the Figure of Eight event, whilst Magesuppe was second in the Wakefield Trophy Contest for cross-country flights. Tiltman's new system of assembly proved its worth in this event. Major Petre won the Rig and Fly Contest for advanced sailplanes, the machine being fully rigged in 3 minutes 37 seconds.

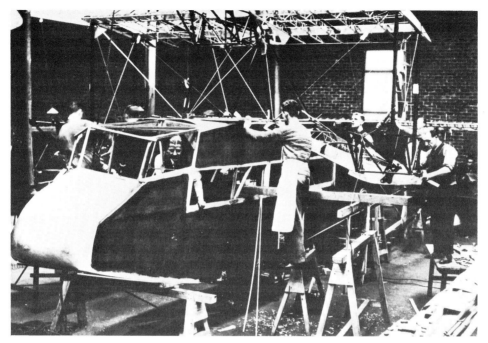

A close-up view of a Ferry under construction at York.   *Airspeed Limited*

The return from Brighton was marked by a little difficulty late at night on the South Downs. The driver of the Buick, which carried the ground crew and towed the trailer, habitually drove at high speed with or without the trailer. Whilst hurtling through the night a violent lurch caused the car to swerve from side to side; when it stopped the trailer had disappeared. It was eventually found in a field minus the nearside wheel. Fortunately the sailplane was not seriously damaged, but the trailer axle had been bought from a scrap merchant, so no replacement was immediately available. The team had no alternative but to carry on to York where an irate Norway had received a telephone call from an equally irate farmer demanding that Airspeed's trailer should be removed immediately, otherwise it would be set on fire.

In its day Tern held all British gliding records. The real significance of these modest achievements was in the fact that Airspeed had been proved capable of building an aircraft which flew well. Local and national publicity stimulated interest.

Two Terns were completed at York. The components of the third were sold, but nothing is known of their fate. In 1934 George Little, brother of David

Little, the company secretary, bought one of the sailplanes. George was one of the earliest recruits in the company and owned the machine until 1947. This was probably the one rebuilt in that year by a Northumberland dental surgeon, who also bought the second aircraft for spares.

The sailplane project was based upon an over-optimistic view of the potential of motorless flight in Britain. The country was not ready for it. Germany's interest was primarily military in character, as a flying training operation sponsored by the Government to evade the restrictions imposed by the Versailles Treaty.

The Tern made no money. Admittedly it had brought more working investors into the business, but the rate at which money was disappearing was most alarming. Norway had commenced his career as a novelist several years before; as the Tern programme ended he had just completed his book *Lonely Road*. He decided that he could no longer afford to write but must devote all his time to the company, and wrote nothing more for five years.

The A.S.4 Ferry prototype was under construction for Cobham as a 55-foot (16.76m) span biplane with three 120 hp engines. One upright DH. Gipsy III was mounted on the centre section of the upper wing and two inverted Gipsy II were on the lower wing. The roomy cabin seated ten passengers. To ensure maximum space inside the fuselage all control runs were outside. An aluminium fairing on the port side gave access for adjustment and servicing. The undercarriage was beyond the manufacturing capacity of the company, so it was sub-contracted to the new Dowty Company and is believed to be the first order for an aircraft undercarriage to be placed with Dowty.

Early in 1932 Norway prepared a brochure on the Ferry which included the following observation:

> "For the last few years there has been a tendency towards increasing speed in the design of civil aircraft. America has led the way in this respect, with fast transcontinental services for passengers and mails, and Europe with its very different circumstances is following. Faster types are coming on the market . . . carrying less payload per horsepower and stalling at a higher speed.
>
> "This process is all to the good, but there is another side to the picture. All speed is expensive, and in these days it is not an easy matter to find purchasers for air transport at all, let alone to find purchasers for very fast air transport. The circumstances of the world are adverse to high speed; if we are to travel we must travel cheaply."

The bus garage in which the Ferry was completed in March 1932, was only 120 feet (36.6m) long and 60 feet (18.3m) wide, with a sliding door at one end. Due to internal obstructions it was not possible to rig the aeroplane completely.

To fit the wings the nose cone and rudder were removed and the fuselage slewed across the shop on specially built bogies.

As York had no aerodrome, flight tests were to be carried out at Sherburn in Elmet, the base of the Yorkshire Aero Club. To avoid the delay of a complete strip and rebuild at Sherburn it was decided to remove the wings, which reduced the overall width to 16 feet (4.9m), fit road wheels to the undercarriage, make a special shoe to mount the tail upon the prime mover of an articulated vehicle and tow it, at night, to the aerodrome.

On the way, under police escort, the bolts holding the tail shoe to the vehicle broke. Fortunately no damage was done as the tail fell to the road. A local garage proprietor was roused from his bed to provide replacement bolts. The convoy proceeded until 2 a.m. when it met the rudder of the liner *Berengaria* travelling north. The air had to give way to the more senior service, so the Ferry was disconnected and manhandled into a side road whilst the liner-less rudder passed by. The aerodrome was reached at dawn and assembly of the aircraft began immediately.

Norway had decided that his experience was inadequate to test the new machine, which represented a substantial capital investment by the company. He arranged for the flights to be carried out by Capt. H. V. Worrall, Chief Pilot of Yorkshire Flying Services, for a fee of £30. On 5th April the engine runs and rigging checks had been satisfactorily concluded. Worrall taxied around the aerodrome for a short time to get the feel of the controls, turned into wind and opened the throttles for a brief lift-off. The Ferry took off after a very short run and Worrall was so pleased with the trim that he flew for nineteen minutes. Minor adjustments were required to correct slight nose heaviness and the rudder balance was excessive.

Hessell Tiltman recalled a newspaper reporter writing about the maiden flight: "He watched with intense interest the face of the designer as an expression of acute anxiety gradually gave way to one of intense relief as the machine safely took the air."

After lunch workspeople were embarked and taken for a flight; presumably the A.I.D. were not present. One passenger was terrified; as the Ferry climbed through the overcast he was gazing in the direction of one of the brilliantly polished engine cowlings when suddenly, as the aircraft broke through the cloud, a shaft of sunlight flashed on the cowling, convincing the nervous passenger that the Ferry had burst into flames.

Further flight trials revealed a slightly longer take off run than had been envisaged. A set of finer pitch propellers cured this. The empty weight was within 24 lb (11 kg) of the estimate. The outcome of the test flights was a tremendous tribute to Tiltman and his team who, as Tiltman said, "built it with no data and no money."

A ludicrous situation developed over an Air Ministry ruling that all aircraft carrying ten passengers must have radio. Tiltman protested that as it would spend its life carrying passengers in the immediate vicinity of aerodromes there could be no possible need for radio. The Air Ministry was adamant; Tiltman and Cobham finally agreed to sacrifice one seat and fit radio. "But," said the Ministry, "if you have only nine seats you do not require radio." Finally common sense prevailed and the radio was omitted.

Sir Alan Cobham had started his National Aviation Day displays at Hanworth Air Park on 12th April and it was essential, in view of the great success of the show, that the first Ferry be delivered as quickly as possible. All new aircraft had to be tested at the R.A.F. Aeroplane and Armament Experimental Establishment at Martlesham Heath before a Certificate of Airworthiness could be issued. The Air Ministry and the R.A.F. at Martlesham cut through red tape and the Ferry passed its tests in four days. On 4th May 1932, the prototype, G-ABSI, named *Youth of Britain II*, joined Sir Alan Cobham's circus at Hanworth in a special display and then immediately went on tour. The second Ferry, G-ABSJ, was under construction and it had been decided to build a further two sets of parts in anticipation of further orders.

By the end of 1935 G-ABSI had flown 1,700 hours, made 17,700 landings and carried approximately 159,300 passengers. Airspeed had, once again, proved the soundness of its technical prowess, but the financial position was causing great concern. The overdraft was over £4,000 and Lord Grimthorpe was called upon weekly to guarantee the wages. Nine shareholders worked in the company, with other interested people investing small sums and working when they could.

The second Ferry, named *Youth of Britain III*, was delivered to Cobham in June 1932. She was damaged in an accident which caused no injuries, and was grounded for several weeks.

In November, the Chief Engineer of National Aviation Day, Mr A. Hutchinson, wrote to Airspeed giving high praise to the two aircraft. He said that during the whole of his career in maintaining similar types he had never found one easier to maintain. In spite of the machines being out in all weather the cost for complete overhaul was expected to be much lower than anticipated.

Two letters received by the company from pilots were most enthusiastic. The Ferry was evidently a pilot's aeroplane, with good full load, short field take-off characteristics and controls so well harmonised that it was no more difficult to fly than a light aircraft. The hydraulic brakes were highly praised, and one pilot concluded with the opinion that few aircraft, if any, could compete with the Ferry's performance.

Norway was of that rare breed, a first-class technical man with a good appreciation of marketing, known as selling in those simple times. He immediately produced a sales brochure including these letters and quoted the economics of the Ferry operated on a service from London to York, a stage length of approximately 180 miles (290 km), and a route efficiently served by the railway. An annual utilisation of 350 hours was assumed.

The cost analysis per flying hour was as follows:—

Petrol and oil	£1 1s.	(£1.05)
Pilot's salary	£1 0s.	(£1.00)
Insurance	£1 0s.	(£1.00)
Maintenance	£0 15s.	(£0.75)
Depreciation at 20%	£2 6s.	(£2.30)
	£6 2s.	(£6.10)

Twelve passengers would fly for two hours at a cost of £12 4s. (£12.20), £1 0s. 4d. (1.01) per person.

The third class rail fare from London to York was £1 3s. 7d. (£1.18), or 3s. 3d. (£0.16) more than travelling by Ferry. Norway appears to have let his enthusiasm outstrip his commercial sense in this brochure, as no allowance was made for airline overheads or profit and there was no reference to the cost and time involved in transit to and from the airfield.

G-ABSJ, after two years with Cobham's Circus, was sold to Himalaya Air Transport and Survey Limited to convey pilgrims to a holy shrine high in the mountains, thus saving four weeks of travel by normal means.

The reliability of the Ferry was proved yet again. Service facilities were primitive in the extreme, the hangar was merely a roof supported on poles about

The prototype Ferry G-ABSI being refuelled at a National Aviation Day display in 1932. The bulge on the side of the nose covers access to the flying controls.

Routine maintenance on Ferry G-ACFB.

twenty feet (6.1m) high. *Dragoman*, as it was named, gave good service until 1936 when the fuselage was found to be infested with white ants. The aeroplane was scrapped.

Two more examples of the Ferry were built, G-ACBT at York and G-ACFB at the new Portsmouth factory to which Airspeed moved in 1933. Both were sold to Midland and Scottish Air Ferries whose managing director, John Sword, was a director of a bus company, Scottish Motor Traction. S.M.T. was also involved in aviation, causing some friction as Sword's operation was a private one.

Sword was planning to operate services between Glasgow and Belfast, Edinburgh, Inverness and the Western Isles. He was also considering a link with Hull to connect with a K.L.M. service from Amsterdam. These projects were too ambitious and symptomatic of the tremendous optimism which marked, and usually ruined, small operators in the Thirties.

M.S.A.F. did, however, operate successful charter flights to the British Industries Fair at Castle Bromwich in 1933 and 1934. They linked London (Heston) and Liverpool with Birmingham.

One of the M.S.A.F. pilots was Capt. J. H. Orrell who, until his retirement, was Chief Test Pilot of A. V. Roe and Company Limited. Capt.

Orrell recalls a flight in G-ACBT to the Western Isles with a charter party when all three engines cut near Oban after 53 minutes. After a descent of 1,500 feet (457m) the engines re-started, but the pilot decided to force-land rather than risk the water crossing or return over the hills to Renfrew. Eventually he flew the Ferry solo to Renfrew and, suspecting the cause of the trouble, flew round the aerodrome for 53 minutes. All three engines cut punctually.

N. S. Norway brought a party to Renfrew armed with gauges which proved negative pressure in the tanks. The tank vents were modified and no further trouble occurred.

Capt. Orrell discussed the problem with Joe King, one of Sir Alan Cobham's pilots. Clearly their flight times were insufficient for this particular trouble to develop. During this conversation they discussed operation from small fields, and Joe King was asked how he coped. "Well," he said, "I taxi like hell to the corner of the field, turn round quick, hold aileron hard one way, when one wheel lifts I snatch it off whilst the other one isn't looking!" Carefree days!

A Midland and Scottish Air Ferries Airspeed Ferry at Stanley Park aerodrome, Blackpool, about to take members of the Blackpool Town Council on their first flight over the Illuminations, 15th September, 1934. The pilot, Captain J. H. Orrell, is second from the right.

Captain J. H. Orrell, O.B.E.

A popular charter operation was a series of flights from Stanley Park, Blackpool, to see the Illuminations. Aerodrome lighting was provided by a searchlight on a lorry.

An intriguing aeronautical theory was propounded when a Ferry was forced to land on Southport sands after a failure of one of the outer engines. Having survived a serious row with the A.I.D. Capt. Orrell went to Southport to fly it home on two engines. When he arrived at site he was surprised to find that the recalcitrant engine had disappeared from the wing, the ground engineer explaining that, to save weight and drag he had carefully stowed it in the cabin. There it remained for the flight to Renfrew. The A.I.D. were even more incensed.

As soon as design work on the Ferry had been completed Tiltman and Norway had begun to think about the next project. Tiltman had been stimulated by an aviation magazine illustration of a new American low wing monoplane with a retractable undercarriage. He decided that an equally advanced concept must be the next project for Airspeed and, fully supported by Norway, produced tentative sketches which received Board approval in November 1931.

Through the summer of 1933 and 1934 the two M.S.A.F. Ferries, attractively painted in white with red trim, flew from Renfrew to Campbeltown, Belfast and Speke.

At the end of 1934 Midland and Scottish was wound up and the Ferries offered for sale. Not until April 1936, was G-ACFB sold to Charles W. A. Scott's Air Display which already operated G-ABSI, the prototype, bought when the Cobham Circus closed in 1935. Scott operated them for one season and they were then flown by Air Publicity Limited.

During the following winter they were re-engined with three inverted Gipsy Major engines and carried joy riders in sprightly fashion for another season. In 1939 the prototype was bought by Portsmouth, Southsea and Isle of Wight Aviation Ltd. It saw very little service on this route. At this time G-ACBT was still awaiting a buyer at Renfrew. G-ABSI had a C. of A. overhaul in December, 1939, and was impressed into the R.A.F. G-ACFB was left picketed out at Heston when its C. of A. expired in November 1938 and ended its days with an Air Training Corps Squadron at Stoke-on-Trent.

So ended the careers of four interesting aeroplanes, the precursors of the Envoy, Oxford, Horsa and Ambassador. Good reliable work-horses, built, as Hessell Tiltman said many times, with no data and no money, but none the worse for that.

CHAPTER TWO

Courier

THE success of the Ferry in its very specialised field was encouraging to the Board and to the workforce, which had now been increased to about fifty. The main advantage of the Ferry was its economy and safety. However, as Norway said, you cannot sell safety, people pay lip-service to it but will not pay anything for it, as Vickers discovered many years later when they tried to interest overseas airlines in the VC.10 airliner.

As soon as the DH. Dragon was announced it was realised that only good luck would sell the Ferry and that maximum effort must now go into the new monoplane, of which many of the detail drawings were ready.

Cobham had, once again, intimated that he might be able to place an order for the prototype. For several years he had been considering the possibility of refuelling aircraft in flight and had reached the stage where he wished to carry

The prototype Courier G-ABXN in flight. Note the wheels protruding when in retracted position.
Flight

out practical tests. Norway and Tiltman were of the opinion that the private owner market was almost saturated and that commercial aviation was likely to develop if there was a small fast aircraft available at a price which was acceptable to the smaller operator. The new design was a good compromise between the commercial requirement and Cobham's potential long-distance, air-refuelled record breaker.

Lord Wakefield, the oil tycoon, was a generous benefactor to aviation and Cobham tried to enlist his support for a record-breaking flight using the new machine, to be known as A.S.5 Courier. It soon became clear that the company could no longer operate from York if the Courier went ahead, so they would have to move to an aerodrome site.

Negotiations were most complex. Cobham was moving from town to town with the National Aviation Day Circus and trying to fit in appointments with Lord Wakefield, whilst Norway chased after the Circus dealing with minor snags on the Ferry, and trying to pin Cobham down in his tent to discuss moving the works and the possibility of an order being placed.

A municipal aerodrome seemed to be a good site, as it was possible that financial support would be available. A number of towns were visited. In April 1932, Cobham placed an order for the Courier, Lord Wakefield having agreed to sponsor the record attempt to the extent of £10,000, made up of £5,000 for the aircraft and £5,000 for the incidental expenses. Mr John Siddeley, of Armstrong Siddeley Motors, made a major contribution in the form of a geared Lynx radial engine.

Lord Ronaldshay, a nephew of Lord Grimthorpe, had become extremely interested in the company and had been working on the shop floor in an unpaid capacity. He suddenly announced that he would invest £1,000 in Airspeed. So the omens for the launch of the Courier were most auspicious.

The design was very advanced for its day. It had been decided that it must be at least up to contemporary American standards and would be the first British commercial aeroplane to have a retractable undercarriage. This caused Hessell

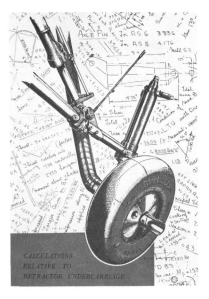

Details of a retractable undercarriage, from the Airspeed Aeronautical College prospectus.

Tiltman considerable trouble. Every part of it had to be designed from scratch and in his diary he complained that "The wretched thing seemed to want to get mixed up with the fuel tank and the flying controls."

Cobham's contract with Airspeed included penalty clauses, one of which stated that the machine would only be accepted if delivered before 1st April 1933. A gestation period of eleven months with not a single component in production provided the company with a formidable task.

Cobham's Circus was rushing indefatigably about the country spreading the gospel of air-mindedness with flights in the Ferry, Avro 504s and a Handley Page W10, all at five bob (25p) a time. In a summer tour of 180 events the Circus was due to visit Yeadon, now Leeds/Bradford Airport, and Sherburn in Elmet, and a further display was to be given in Middleton Park within the Leeds City boundary. How uncomplicated aviation was in those halcyon days! Even the Tiger Moth was referred to in the local paper as a "plane specially designed for the advanced training of Service pilots".

Cobham's theory was that his operations would give a boost to the success of internal airlines and would create a demand for them and thus for the Courier and Ferry. The Leeds M.P., Mr Noel Whiteside, arranged for a local businessman to be flown to a number of centres to demonstrate how air travel saves time. One man who was really convinced by these displays was Edward Hillman, a Romford coach operator to whom Airspeed hoped to sell Ferries.

Hillman used the price quoted by Airspeed as a stick to belabour de Havilland into producing an aeroplane to meet his precise requirements. So the DH.84 Dragon was born, and the Ferry was left without a future, a situation which left the prosperity, indeed the very existence of Airspeed, dependent upon the Courier.

Tiltman found himself up against the classic problem of aircraft designers, how to reconcile two almost irreconcilable design requirements; a long-range aircraft, in other words, a flying petrol tank with petrol as far aft as possible, and a cabin machine seating six passengers as far forward as possible. Norway was rightly insistent upon avoiding any alterations to the passenger machine to meet Cobham's requirements, so keeping the centre of gravity in the right position was extremely difficult. Another problem which Tiltman discussed with the Royal Aircraft Establishment at Farnborough at great length was the phenomenon of buffeting which had seemed to be characteristic of most low wing cantilver monoplanes built to date, few though they were.

After lengthy discussions with various municipal authorities, the Board decided that an offer from Portsmouth was a most attractive one and that the company would transfer its operations to the South Coast. Portsmouth aerodrome was very suitably located on the shore of Langstone Harbour, which had been designated as a major terminal for the flying boat services throughout the Commonwealth expected to commence as soon as the new Short Empire

An air display at Portsmouth aerodrome in 1933, showing the new Airspeed factory.   *Flight*

boats were in service. The town had a good engineering labour force and the council was anxious to reduce its total dependence upon the Naval Dockyard, being prepared to build the factory and spread 75 per cent of the cost to Airspeed over ten years. Even this generous offer was fraught with financial peril but, at the September Board meeting, the decision to go ahead was minuted.

So the die was cast, and the major operation of moving a complete production unit and a half-completed Courier being built to a very tight time schedule was planned in detail. Portsmouth was the eighth largest municipal aerodrome in the country. Opened on 2nd July 1932, by Sir Philip Sassoon, the Under-Secretary of State for Air, it had a landing area of 204 acres, with grass strips 4,500 feet (1372m) and 2,400 feet (732m) long. The opening was a gala event, with over 100 visiting aircraft and an air display watched by 50,000 people. The *Graf Zeppelin* marked the occasion by diverting to fly over the display and, no doubt, have a look at the Naval Dockyard. The local flying club offered flying lessons and an 'A' Licence cost £30. In August Sir Alan Cobham took his Flying Circus to Portsmouth and took members of the Corporation for trips in the Ferry. He commented that it was the best aerodrome from which he had operated.

On the day the negotiations were completed Norway and Lord Grimthorpe were entertained by the Lord Mayor to lunch in the Guildhall. Whilst waiting for a train to London they had tea in a small café. Norway, most excited over the decisions, rated the council's offer as a "model of the sort of encouragement that can be given by an enterprising city to an infant industry." His elation was short lived, for Lord Grimthorpe gravely expressed his misgivings over the retractable undercarriage planned for the Courier. Having a large financial stake in the company, he naturally would take every step open to him to ensure that no mistakes were made. He had shown the Courier drawings to a friend who, in turn, had shown them to a very eminent aircraft designer. Norway never revealed who it was, all that is known is that it was either Sydney Camm, of Hawkers, who designed the Hurricane, or R. J. Mitchell, of Supermarines, who designed the Spitfire. The eminent designer had advised that the retractable undercarriage was a great mistake, it could not be made to work reliably, imposed a weight penalty and would make little difference to the performance of the aeroplane.

Norway was shattered. He stuck doggedly to his guns and told the chairman that Airspeed must lead the way. Simply to follow in the footsteps of the larger companies and produce an aircraft in direct competition would inevitably mean that Airspeed would not have the advantages of their volume production and the unfavourable economics would lead inevitably to failure. They could not possibly compete on price, so must do so on innovation and technical advance. Lord Grimthorpe was convinced and the retractable undercarriage remained in the Specification.

It is interesting to consider the implications of this decision on the outcome of the Battle of Britain. Would the Hurricane and Spitfire have had retractable undercarriages if Airspeed had not built the Courier and proved the great advantage to be gained? The progenitor of the Spitfire, the F7/30, certainly had a fixed undercarriage, so Mitchell might well have been the sceptic.

In the last months at York a contract was placed with Airspeed to build a single-seat parasol monoplane for W. S. Shackleton and Lee Murray, who had designed it to be fitted with a German Hirth engine. It was considered that it might have a future in the private owner market.

By the end of 1932 most of the detail drawings of the Courier had been issued to the shops and construction was proceeding. The fuselage was of mixed construction. Aft of the engine bay bulkhead spruce frames and longerons were covered with stressed plywood. Forward of the bulkhead a steel tubular structure formed the engine mounting.

The wings were twin-spar wooden cantilever outer panels bolted to the main centre section structure, which carried the retractable undercarriage units mounted with the axles supported on abutments when in the retracted position, so that the wheels partially projected below the wing and would support the aircraft in the event of a wheels-up landing. Only minimal damage would then result. The Lynx engine was to be cowled with a Townend ring cowling, which, combined with the advantages of the retractable undercarriage, was expected to give an extremely high performance to outclass all contemporary aircraft in its category.

As no British aircraft since the Bristol Racer in 1922 had installed such an undercarriage, no company could provide components. Hessell Tiltman was forced to design the installation from first principles and make everything,

The Bristol Racer of 1922, with its retractable undercarriage. No other British aircraft would have such an undercarriage until the appearance of the Courier.

including the hydraulic rams. A hand pump in the cockpit operated the system and coloured lights indicated the position of the wheels. The system turned out to be extremely effective and reliable.

The fuselage was supported on trestles in the works and Tom Laing, the works manager, spent many hours underneath the Courier eliminating teething troubles with the hydraulics.

Considerable newspaper publicity had followed Sir Alan Cobham's announcement that he intended to attempt a record-breaking flight to Australia in the Courier, and the Board decided that a further Prospectus should be issued in an attempt to increase capital. One thousand copies were issued and only a few hundred pounds materialised.

Fortunately, as Cobham had predicted, the autumn of 1932 had seen awakened interest in internal passenger services, operated, surprisingly, by road transport companies. Norway went to Inverness to negotiate with John Sword the sale of the third Ferry, which was being completed as a speculation. In the midst of dire financial troubles, Tiltman had a telegram from him confirming that Sword had placed an order on condition that he could part-exchange his 6 ½ litre Bentley at a value of £900. Norway would drive this luxurious vehicle to York as the deposit on the contract price.

This deal was crucial to the company, as de Havilland had just flown the first Dragon for Edward Hillman and Tiltman was extremely worried that Sword might buy a Dragon. The Shackleton-Lee Murray lightweight was nearing completion, with the cost escalating far beyond the anticipated level to a figure which gave no confidence in its commercial future.

The contract with Portsmouth City Council for the new factory was signed and a notice appeared on the works notice board stating that the company would move to Portsmouth in the spring of 1933. "In the present difficult circumstances", stated the notice, "the Company can pay no removal or travelling expenses of any sort to any employee. This applies to all grades including Directors . . . If any employee wishes the Secretary to keep back a portion of his pay to provide for the unavoidable personal expenses which will have to be incurred, he should see Mr Little about it."

The cost of the new factory was the only pleasant surprise to be enjoyed by the Board on the financial front. It cost £4,170 instead of the budgeted £4,700 for 14,000 square feet (1,200.64 sq m) of floor area.

On completion of the design work on the Courier several draughtsmen had to be dismissed. To add to their troubles the centre engine and fuel tank on

The prototype Courier on the ground, showing the retractable undercarriage, Lynx engine and Townend ring cowling. *The Aeroplane*

Sword's Ferry was a new design, and everything fouled due to unsatisfactory work on the part of a draughtsman. Delivery was, of course, set back, and this in turn affected the Courier.

The Royal Aircraft Establishment at Farnborough was in a mild dilemma over the stressing of the wing. There was little data on cantilever wings and it was not easy to determine whether the deflection of the wing due to flight loads imposed a similar deflection on both front and rear spars. The influence of the retractable undercarriage on stress levels was not clearly established.

It was finally decided that R.A.E. would send a team to York with a lorry full of sand bags. The wing would then be proof loaded and the deflections measured under simulated flight loads. The fuel tanks were also a major headache due to the 100 foot (30.5m) pressure head during refuelling.

Cobham's delivery deadline and penalty clause were poised like the sword of Damocles. A casual meeting with Armstrong Siddeley at Coventry revealed to

The de Havilland D.H.84 Dragon, which provided such strong competition for the Airspeed aircraft.

Tiltman that the oil filter installed on the Lynx was adequate for a mere ten hours flying; Cobham required 100 hours, so a large filter had to be installed in the cabin, together with the appropriate plumbing and consequent weight and space penalty. The Townend ring cowling had not been started and would not be delivered in time for the first flight.

The fuel system problems were solved, however. The machine carried 275 gallons of petrol in five wing tanks, two being installed in the outer panels. The middle tank in the centre section was the receiver tank. This was fitted with a jettison valve so that, in an emergency, this tank could be quickly emptied, the contents of the other tanks would flow into the centre tank and be jettisoned at a slower rate. A five-inch (127mm) diameter vent pipe was required to ensure that pressure could, under no circumstances, rupture the tanks. When carrying the full fuel load for the Australia flight the gross weight was 5,050 lb (2971 kg) with a maximum take-off weight of 3,500 lb (2,427 kg). A duration of 25 hours and a range of nearly 3,000 miles (4,830 k/m) was specified.

In March, 1933, the company moved in a convoy of lorries to the new Portsmouth factory. Someone irreverently suggested that each lorry should have a man on its tailboard armed with a shotgun to repel bailiffs!

Of the hundred men working at York only 50 moved south. Later some of those who could not find jobs and were doubtless influenced by the prospect of better weather followed on, and did not return to the North. So Airspeed built up a competent and stable labour force in a short time. At last the whole of the Airspeed team was under one roof, with a fine aerodrome outside the door. They had a working area three times the size of the York premises and were cautiously optimistic that lower costs could be achieved.

Cobham's Courier was almost complete when the move took place. It only required rectification of slight damage caused in transit before it was ready for testing.

The choice of a test pilot caused Norway much concern. The future of the company and all its staff depended upon the Courier, and any error or accident at this critical stage would mean ruin. The move had played havoc with finances, so a large fee for one of the major civilian test pilots was not practicable. Norway contacted Flight Lieutenant G. H. Stainforth, a serving officer in the R.A.F. based at the Royal Aircraft Establishment. He held the World Speed Record in the Schneider Trophy Supermarine S6b and was one of the finest test pilots in the country. He was very interested in the Courier and had no difficulty in obtaining permission from his superiors to fly it. So, for a pittance, George Stainforth was committed to this very responsible task. The retractable undercarriage had been thoroughly tested statically but in flight loading conditions was an unknown quantity.

The first flight, without the Townend ring cowling, surprised even Hessell Tiltman, who had calculated a top speed at sea level of 155 m.p.h. (249 km/hr). Farnborough had predicted 145 m.p.h. (233 km/hr). The actual figure was 163 m.p.h. (262 km/hr). The difference in speed with the undercarriage up and down was 37 m.p.h. (60 km/hr), far greater than envisaged.

The Courier handled extremely well, and Stainforth was very impressed. He flew it for about five hours, and by masterly flying saved it from disaster. He was taking off over Langstone Harbour and was at 300 feet (91 m), climbing steeply with the wheels up, when suddenly the engine failed. Stainforth reacted instantly, the nose went down to maintain speed and the wheels went down as he turned gently down wind and landed smoothly on the aerodrome.

On another occasion an engine failure caused a rather rough landing outside the aerodrome. Both radius rods collapsed, but miraculously they jammed against the structure in a manner which prevented total undercarriage collapse and serious damage.

Stainforth completed the initial performance trials and established figures which were precisely the same as the figures issued by Farnborough after the subsequent trials at Martlesham Heath. Later in the year Norway and Tiltman were flying with another pilot to Brooklands to demonstrate the aircraft when a hydraulic connection failed. Fortunately it was accessible in the air and Norway, in the second seat, was able to hold the two parts together whilst the undercarriage was pumped down and locked.

The aeroplane was blessed with good fortune in these critical early stages. A Martlesham pilot, making a short flight, pumped the wheels down till the lights showed green and gave two more pumps "for luck". Suddenly the lever was useless; as he had green lights he landed, doing so safely. It was found that a screwdriver had been driven into one of the flexible hydraulic hoses and had almost penetrated the wall. The extra two pump operations were too much for it. A similar occurrence on retraction would have meant a belly landing.

The Martlesham trials were extended, the Air Ministry being very interested in this new aircraft which was to have an impact on the design of military aircraft.

Cobham's projected flight to Australia had been widely publicised in the national press and the Courier had been the subject of very favourable comment, but still orders did not materialise.

The move to Portsmouth and the consequent disruption of production had been expensive. The Board had decided to lay down a production line of six Couriers and the overdraft had risen to £10,000. Lord Grimthorpe's action in

The men behind the Courier, with the Courier behind them. Right to left, Lord Grimthorpe, A. Hessell Tiltman, Nevil Shute Norway. On left, Flight Lieutenant C.H.S.Colman. *Flight*

taking up another £1,000 of shares and giving a personal guarantee of another £5,000 prompted a bold and generous gesture on the part of the group of working shareholders who were not members of the Board. They were so convinced that the company would prosper that they collectively, without consulting Tiltman or Norway, offered the Company a further £12,000 in the form of debentures. Every few months Hessell Tiltman's diary recorded the emergence of someone who was considering a large or small investment in the company, but rarely did any money appear.

A disturbing mishap to the Courier prototype at Martlesham in June caused Tiltman to give very serious consideration to current Farnborough undercarriage stressing requirements. Flight Lieutenant Boothman was carrying out a series of "stick" and "unstick" tests at an all-up weight of 3,700 lb (1,678 kg) when, whilst taxiing for take-off at 15 m.p.h., the port undercarriage collapsed. The machine settled down quite gently and dug the aileron balance into the ground. It could hardly have happened at a worse time, for Norway was in negotiation with Squadron Leader Brady, of Aircraft Exchange and Mart, who was interested in taking the selling agency, and Brady was due to visit Martlesham that day. Tiltman hastily 'phoned Norway and Brady was stopped just in time.

Further inspection revealed that little damage had resulted from the mishap. A radius rod had failed, although it had been stressed to take twice the load specified by Farnborough. The machine was flying again within a few days, and Brady was so impressed with it ultimately that he took the sole agency for the United Kingdom and placed the first order for a demonstrator.

The trials created a minor sensation in the Air Ministry, and leading aircraft designers were invited to see the Courier whilst it was at Martlesham; Norway saw this as an exercise in "rubbing their noses in it."

Cobham's delivery deadline of 1st April had been overtaken by events. His own arrangements had fallen way behind due to his business commitments delaying the negotiation of landing rights in the various countries en route to Australia.

C. G. Grey, editor of *The Aeroplane*, a formidable critic, wrote about the Courier, "One of the best-looking jobs I have ever seen. Paint and prettiness have sold more motor cars than price or performance, and the latest Cellon finish on the Courier, which is done in dark and pale blue with scarlet lettering, can be put up against any multiple coated hand polished and varnished American aeroplane that has ever been seen.

"Prettiness of line goes a long way and the old motto, 'if a thing looks right it is right', still holds. The lines of the Courier definitely are beautiful. When you see it sliding through the air at about 150 m.p.h. with the undercarriage neatly tucked up into the wings it strikes you at once that it looks as an aeroplane should.

"Messrs Norway and Tiltman, in spite of being slide rule experts and

Cobham's Courier being refuelled from the Handley Page W.10 tanker. These early experiments led to present-day techniques used by the Royal Air Force, the U.S. Air Force and others.

Flight Refuelling Limited

practical engineers are inherently artists. They evidently are not only able to calculate the stresses which the machine has to take, and to design parts and fittings to take those stresses, but they seem to have the unusual faculty of being able to see the spray! Everything on the machine is faired off in the right way."

Grey concluded his two-page article "The construction and workmanship are all they should be and is a credit to the production engineering. The Courier deserves all the success it is bound to get and it is bound to get it because Airspeed now offer the world something which in its own class is definitely better than is being offered by any other country." Unfortunately Grey's enthusiasm was not manifest in the market place. The DH. Dragon was forging ahead. By the end of September 1933, 55 Dragons were in service all over the world, a remarkable achievement in less than two years.

On 4th September, "Bones" Brady, of Aircraft Exchange and Mart, took delivery of their demonstrator, G-ACJL; two other machines were being built. Cobham, with Squadron Leader W. Helmore, was developing flight refuelling techniques for the long-delayed flight to Australia in G-ABXN, whilst Tiltman

A view from the W.10 tanker of Squadron Leader W. Helmore in the Courier receiving the hose for connection to the collector tank. In 1933 this was a task requiring nerve as well as skill.

Flight

was feeling frustrated by the work the factory was called upon to do on the Handley Page W 10 which was to be the tanker aircraft.

The W 10, G-EBMR, normally used in Cobham's Circus, was stripped of its seating and a track built inside. Standard fuel drums were rolled down the track and, in the aftermost position, connected to the trailing hose, the end of which was attached to a trail rope. The Courier had a large hatch in the cabin top, and, once the machine had formated about 50 feet (15.2m) below and astern of the tanker, Helmore would stand up in the hatch and catch the trail rope preparatory to hauling in the hose for connection to the collector tank.

An early test almost ended in disaster. The four-pound (1.8 kg) weight on the trail rope was near to the Courier with Helmore trying to catch it. Cobham banked slightly to bring it within reach, when suddenly the machine was in a violent sideslip with a jammed aileron control. The weight had entered the aileron gap and wedged itself solidly in position on the port side. Attempts to centralise the stick and stabilise the Courier only jammed the controls more tightly, height was being lost at an alarming rate and six turns of a spiral dive had been completed before it was realised what had happened. Cobham threw the stick violently to starboard and the weight dropped out, but by that time the aircraft was perilously close to the ground.

A simple modification avoided risk of further trouble. A child's balloon was filled with water and connected to the rope by a very light cord.

In this primitive way was developed the technique which put Flight Refuelling Limited right in the forefront of its business. Today it builds equipment to refuel supersonic aircraft in flight.

Cobham's many short development flights were of great value in eliminating teething troubles with the Courier, troubles which were quite trivial but would have been a major annoyance to customers, but Tiltman and Norway were becoming very impatient with Cobham who, they felt, was not concentrating all his energies on the project. In October 1933, Tiltman wrote a rather testy letter to Sir Alan in which he said "... The main point which I want to raise is the somewhat haphazard manner in which the work of perfecting the re-fuelling technique is being carried out. We feel most definitely that the work is not such as can be handled in a number of short periods of time spread out at very long intervals. In our considered opinion it is work—more or less of a research nature—which requires much patient thought and attention to detail. It is work which cannot be carried out in a hurry in periods between lunch and tea."

The demonstration Courier built for R. K. Dundas, Airspeed's distributor in India, seen with a contemporary Rolls-Royce.   *Airspeed Limited*

He went on to suggest that Cobham should recruit two pilots to relieve him and Helmore of the hack work. Sadly, Sir Alan's reply to this letter has not survived.

Orders were still few and far between. Some were from optimistic and impecunious entrepreneurs who believed that aviation was the coming thing and that the best way to get into it was to order an aeroplane on hire purchase and hope for the best. In September Aircraft Exchange and Mart flew their demonstrator to Renfrew at an average speed of 131 m.p.h. (211 km/hr) to show its capabilities to John Sword, of Midland and Scottish Air Ferries, who already operated the two Airspeed Ferry transports. No success was achieved, and M.A.S.A.F. were to terminate operations at the end of September.

Lord Ronaldshay had contacts in India and was convinced that a market existed there. He and R. D. King, sales manager of Airspeed, formed R. K. Dundas Limited to market Airspeed machines in India and Burma and a demonstrator, G-ACLF, was built for them. This was fitted with a 305 h.p. Armstrong Siddeley Cheetah V seven-cylinder radial engine to give adequate power in tropical climates. In December 1933, G-ACLF, with C. E. Kelly at the controls and Lord Ronaldshay as co-pilot, left Portsmouth for Delhi via Paris, Marseilles, Catania, Tunis, Tripoli and Cairo. The flight was uneventful. Only one Courier was sold in India, to the Maharajah of Jaipur.

Recalling his part in the sale of this aeroplane, David D. Little, company secretary at the time, tells how after the long journey out from England and a three-day wait for an audience with the Maharajah, he found the customer more interested in paint than performance. He asked very little about the aircraft, but said that it must be painted in his house colours, which could be seen on one of his Rolls-Royces.

Three Couriers were ordered by Stanley Bell, of London, Scottish & Provincial Airways Limited. Two were delivered and based at Sherburn in Elmet, where the Ferry had first flown. The route was from Sherburn to Paris, via Nottingham and London, and the flight time, including stops, was less than three hours. It was hoped to extend the service to Glasgow.

The Couriers were supplied on hire purchase and the struggling airline was always in financial trouble, as indeed was almost the whole of the industry at that time. Just before a take-off for Paris, two bowler-hatted gentlemen appeared and told Bell that they had instructions to impound the aeroplane in settlement of a fuel bill for £300. Bell was somewhat nonplussed as he had three passengers in the cabin, but he rose to the occasion and suggested to the bailiffs that they should at least have a look at the machine they were to impound. They took the bait and climbed inside. Bell immediately slammed the door and took off. On arrival at Paris the unwilling passengers were promptly taken into custody for arriving without passports, whilst the Courier went about its normal business.

The oil company to whom the money was owed was so amused by the incident that it gave the airline a further three months credit.

An Air Ministry order for a Courier was a major event for Airspeed, as they were not members of that very select ring, the Society of British Aircraft Constructors, and not, therefore, eligible for military orders.

Finance was a recurrent nightmare, and to add to their problems, a major extension to the factory had been agreed with the Portsmouth Corporation. Hessell Tiltman was most upset on one occasion when, on entering his office, Norway said, "Tiltman, we are in serious trouble, today is Thursday, tomorrow

The assembly shop at Portsmouth in January, 1934. Courier G-ACNZ for use as test bed for the Napier Rapier engine can be seen on the left, and K.4047 for the Air Ministry is just visible at rear right. *Airspeed Limited*

we must pay the wages, we are over our limit with the bank, I have approached the directors jointly and severally and none will cough up another penny."

Tiltman was aghast. "What do we do then?" "It is quite simple," said Norway, "there is only one thing to do. Will you immediately send for the man who collects the wages and we will brief him."

The man appeared. "Now, I want you to listen very carefully," said Norway. "We have financial difficulties with the bank, you will take the pay cheque in the normal way, whistling blithely as if you haven't a care in the world, put the cheque on the counter and say 'Wages please!' When you have the money move out as quickly as possible.''

The money was handed over without demur. Fortunately a Courier was sold during the next week, and the financial problem was sorted out for the time being.

The next year, 1934, saw an improvement in sales of the Courier, and Cobham's flight to Australia had been rescheduled to terminate in India. Portsmouth, Southsea and Isle of Wight Aviation ordered two Couriers for their local services. Ultimately they operated five, one of which, G-ACVF, was still flying with East Anglian Flying Services in 1949.

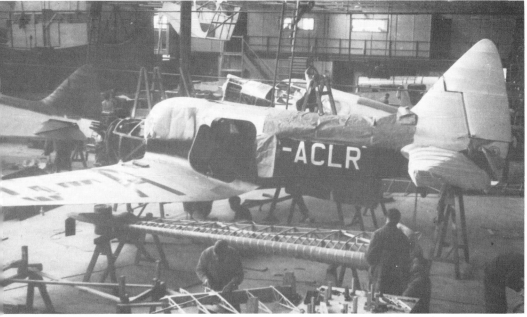

Another view of the assembly shop at the Portsmouth works, with Courier G-ACLR under construction. The Napier Rapier test bed G-ACNZ is visible in the background, while in the foreground work goes on to construct the wings of another aircraft. *Airspeed Limited*

D. Napier and Son, who were in 1933 developing their Rapier sixteen-cylinder H-type engine, ordered a Courier as a test bed and demonstrator for the 350 h.p. Mk IV Rapier. Delivered in June 1934, it was usually flown by Air Vice-Marshal A. E. Borton, a director of Napier's. Trouble with oil and cylinder head temperatures was dealt with in a simple manner. When it was found that prolonged taxiing to the take-off point caused overheating, pilots adopted the procedure of switching off for 15 minutes and then restarting the engine for a quick take-off, reaching an adequate air speed before further trouble developed.

The Rapier had an unusually small frontal area, which improved the performance but certainly not the appearance of the Courier. A four-bladed propeller and a massive array of exhaust plumbing gave it a rather ungainly appearance. G-ACNZ was entered in the 1934 King's Cup Race, Air Vice-Marshal Borton averaging 166 m.p.h. (267 km/hr) before elimination in the heats; the handicappers were too brutal to give him a chance of success.

A memorable flight carried out by Air Vice-Marshal Borton with that inveterate traveller Sir Harry Brittain took them to Moscow as guests of the Soviet Government. This resulted from a dinner party gaffe by Sir Harry, who expressed to one of his fellow guests, in quite uncompromising terms, his opinion of the Soviet regime. The other guest was Mr Ivan Maisky, the Russian Ambassador, who invited him to dinner at the Embassy to discuss their political differences.

Sir Harry mentioned his invitation to visit Russia to Air Vice-Marshal Borton, whom he knew well. Borton instantly suggested that the quickest way would be to use the Courier, and an opportunity could arise to study Soviet aviation. So they set off by way of Amsterdam, Berlin and Danzig, receiving a civic welcome at Kaunas, the capital of Lithuania. Between Kaunas and Moscow conditions were appalling, torrential rain and hail doing its best to batter the Courier into the treetops. There was no problem with engine temperatures!

Borton's skill and the reliability of the Courier and its relatively new engine brought them safely to a warm welcome in Moscow. Their visit to an aircraft

The Napier Rapier Courier G-ACNZ when taking part in the King's Cup air race heats in July, 1934. Left to right are Air Vice-Marshall A. E. Borton, Messrs. Winter, Smith and Savage.

Aeroplane Monthly

factory prompted Sir Harry to comment on ''their little touch of gallery by-play'' when he noticed the pots of hydrangeas carefully placed between groups of workers. They left Moscow with a collection of souvenirs including a three-foot hydrangea which became airborne in every bump. Sir Harry fielded most efficiently at short slip.

By September 1934 Sir Alan Cobham and Squadron Leader Helmore were ready to commence their non-stop flight to India. Development trials had been carried out at Ford aerodrome, near Arundel in Sussex, where a very successful demonstration of flight refuelling had been given to senior R.A.F. and Air Ministry staff including Air Marshal Sir Hugh Dowding. The Courier was at the Portsmouth factory being completely stripped in preparation for the flight to India when Dowding suddenly announced that he could not authorise further support from the Ministry without a further demonstration flight. Norway was furious, but Cobham was not unduly dismayed. He borrowed one of the company's unsold Couriers, installed a temporary fuel system and gave a flawless demonstration in foul weather conditions. Dowding and his colleagues were very impressed.

The take-off was scheduled for dawn on September 21. The Handley Page W 10 tanker was positioned at Ford and a further W 10 was in readiness for refuelling at Malta. Depressions and squalls were reported over France, with poor visibility, so the take-off was postponed for 24 hours. On the next day the

Flight Lieutenant C. H. S. Colman flying the Napier Rapier engined Courier.   *Flight*

Lord Mayor of Portsmouth and other civic dignitaries arrived at a very early hour, and Cobham and Helmore joined them for an official breakfast in the chalet erected for the occasion.

When Hessell Tiltman arrived at 5.30 a.m. he found panic and feverish activity. When the engine of 'XN had been started earlier it had been discovered that the revolution counter was not working, no spare was available and seconds were precious if Malta was to be reached before dark.

Alan Cobham was almost alone in being unperturbed. Everyone else was rushing around and interfering with the others. Jimmy Watson, the works foreman, and Wilson of the A.I.D. discovered that the instrument had been

A de Havilland D.H.89 Dragon Rapide in post-war service with British European Airways. Backed by the de Havilland sales organisation, these aircraft competed strongly with Airspeed's products.
British European Airways

disconnected internally in carrying out Tiltman's instruction to drill a small hole in the casing to release any engine oil which had entered via the flexible drive. In 20 minutes the problem had been solved and the Courier, lightly loaded, took off for its rendezvous with the tanker near Selsey Bill.

Eighty gallons of fuel was transferred and the tanker, G-EBMR, returned to Ford for the removal of the refuelling gear, the Courier continuing to Malta where the other W 10, G-EBMM, was waiting at Halfar airfield. At 4.15 p.m. G.M.T. contact was made and fuel transferred.

After a contents check by Squadron Leader Helmore a second transfer was made. At that point Cobham discovered that the throttle control was no longer effective and the butterfly valve in the carburettor was spring loaded fully open, but closing very slowly. There was no alternative to abandoning the flight and making a hazardous landing, grossly overloaded with fuel, at Halfar.

Cobham decided to leave the wheels in the retracted position and just managed to get into the airfield before all power was lost. In spite of a landing weight of 4,500 lb (2,041 kg) with full tanks, very little damage was caused to the machine, only the propeller being seriously damaged.

The reason for the failure was trivial. All the major problems of refuelling in flight had been overcome as the flight to Malta had proved; a split pin locking a pivot pin in the throttle control linkage had fallen out and the pivot pin itself had soon vibrated out and was found in the bottom of the cowling. A close investigation afterwards proved that no fewer than five people had checked the offending pin, so it was concluded that vibration had worn or fatigued it to the point of failure.

On landing Cobham was shocked to learn that the tanker, G-EBMR, on a positioning flight from Ford to Coventry to rejoin the National Aviation Day display, had crashed after the failure of a tailplane bracing wire. The machine burned and Flight Lieutenant Bremridge and his crew of three died in the wreck. The W 10 had carried 100,000 fare-paying passengers for the Cobham Circus without injury. Sir Alan decided to return immediately with Helmore.

By the autumn of 1933 the experience gained with the Courier in service had indicated that the smaller internal and cross-Channel airlines would be interested in a larger twin-engined machine. Tiltman considered that one could be designed using major components of the Courier such as wing outer panels and tail surfaces. The aircraft would meet the requirements of legislation soon to come into force and would provide strong competition for their old rival de Havilland, who had developed the Dragon into the elegant and efficient DH. 89 Dragon Rapide, being marketed throughout the world with de Havilland's customary panache and efficiency.

At a Board meeting the unsatisfactory financial position was, as usual, at the top of the agenda. Norway proposed that as the only chance of survival for the company was to grow rapidly, they should be bold, build Couriers in batches of six and proceed with the prototype of a new design. To do this would require more factory space, and he recommended an approach to the Corporation to double the size of the factory.

The Board, impressed with Norway's reasoning, concurred. The Corporation agreed to develop the site further and another major stage in the company's growth had begun.

During 1934 the Courier had received useful press publicity when the Marquess of Donegal, with two friends and a ground engineer, chartered a Courier for an "air cruise" around Europe. They visited le Touquet, Paris, Marseilles, Cannes, Rome, Naples, Brindisi, Athens, Salonika, Sofia, Bucharest, Belgrade, Budapest, Vienna, Dresden, Nuremberg, Munich, Salzburg, Leipzig, Berlin, Hamburg and Copenhagen, covering, as Donegal put it, "5,000 miles in perfect comfort with time to look around in twenty-three of the chief towns in Europe." The total cost of the trip was £500.

It was pointed out in the last of the four half-page reports on the trip, in the *Sunday Dispatch*, that a similar journey could be enjoyed on normal airline services for a travel cost of approximately £40. Later in the year rather more disagreeable publicity resulted when a Courier operated by London, Scottish and Provincial Airways Limited on a twice-daily service between Leeds, Nottingham, Heston and Paris crashed in bad weather on high ground near Sevenoaks. The pilot and his three passengers were killed.

The pilot appeared to have lost control in cloud, entered a high-speed dive and attempted a violent recovery which caused structural failure, the machine diving vertically into a road. Tiltman was extremely upset about this accident, the first to harm passengers in an Airspeed machine. Tests were carried out to check the structural integrity of the Courier, but nothing was found which suggested that the crash was caused by anything but pilot error.

The end of 1933 saw a high honour conferred upon Tiltman and Norway, both being elected Fellows of the Royal Aeronautical Society in recognition of their work on the Courier and its retractable undercarriage. Even the Society of British Aircraft Constructors was becoming friendly. The S.B.A.C. was a tightly closed shop enjoying a deal negotiated with a post-war Government at a time when the industry was in the doldrums and which ensured that only member firms would receive contracts for military aircraft. They admitted Airspeed as associate members, allowed them to show the Courier at the S.B.A.C. Display and ultimately admitted them to full membership.

With major expansion of the company it was felt that a full-time test pilot was now necessary. The problem was to find a good man who would join them at the miserly £400 per annum which was all they could afford. Norway had met Flight Lieutenant C. H. A. Colman, who had flown Ferries with Midland and

The front cover of the Airspeed Aeronautical College prospectus, drawn by Concord and Cavendish Morton.

Courier G-ACLS after engine failure over Langstone Harbour. *Airspeed Limited*

Scottish and was flying a Fox Moth for John Sword. He was impressed when he saw Colman pacing out the length of a field into which he had flown his Fox Moth to ensure that there was adequate room to fly it out safely. He thought that this showed a responsible attitude, not always shared by young R.A.F. officers at that time, and one which would be most valuable in a test pilot. Norway approached him and was delighted when Colman agreed to join them.

The year 1934 also saw the takeover of the company by Swan Hunter and Wigham Richardson, the Tyneside shipbuilders. The story is told in the next chapter.

The Board believed that the time had come to invest in home-bred talent and opened the Airspeed Aeronautical College, which offered a three-year course for 250 guineas on a non-residential basis. The Prospectus dated 14th August 1934, had an introduction by Sir Alan Cobham and a paragraph on the subject of ''Deportment''.

''It may not be amiss to emphasise this very important characteristic. The worth of a person to industry or to the common weal is easily discernible by his attitude to work and his general bearing. If he is quick and decisive in his methods it can be safely assumed that he will progress quickly, but the lethargic indolent person who needs urging to work or effort will never assume any position of responsibility.

''The essence of any training is keenness, with this attribute knowledge will surely grow even if at first the task may appear difficult. It is wise to remember that people responsible for training find it more pleasant to teach those who have this characteristic and pleasant training spells success,'' an improving homily which bears the stamp of Norway. The college produced some first-class engineers of immense value in the rapid expansion of the company during the war.

Courier K.4047 built for the Air Ministry ready for a flight test in February, 1934.   *Flight*

The problem of obtaining orders was still a major one. Aircraft Exchange and Mart had not been successful, so R. K. Dundas took over U.K. sales as well as their Indian and Burmese franchise. Most customers of substance went to de Havillands, still a formidable competitor, leaving Airspeed with the impecunious ones of no interest to de Havilland.

The Air Ministry placed an order with the company for the conversion of their Courier K 4047 to investigate the behaviour of a special flap installation. The Courier "floated" to a disconcerting degree on landing. Under the fuselage and centre section Schrenk flaps were fitted, with Handley Page flaps outboard to the ailerons which, themselves, were interconnected to droop as the flaps were lowered but retained their effectiveness as ailerons.

This scheme was a major advance in low-speed control. A steeper approach made landings much easier to judge, whilst the extra lift of the Handley Page flaps permitted a useful reduction in landing speed. Pilots were impressed with the Courier's ability to carry out gliding turns at very low speed with complete stability and safety.

The Courier had now to be considered obsolescent. By the end of 1934 ten had been built and a further six were completed before production ceased in May 1935. Nine of the machines flew during the Second World War and gave good service as taxi aircraft with Air Transport Auxiliary.

The one which survived the war, G-ACVF, was bought by East Anglian Flying Services in March 1947. Captain H. A. M. Pascoe, A.F.C. recalled it with some affection, as the fuselage was almost identical with the Oxford in which he flew for 2,000 hours as an instructor. The aircraft was used mainly for pleasure flights, and to fly passengers to and from Ostend via Lympne. The passengers would buy carpets which were not available in U.K. On one occasion the aircraft was so full of carpets that the out of trim condition resulted in the landing at

Southend being effected by a series of gigantic hops across the airfield. Towards the end of its life the engine was throwing out so much oil that landings had to be made by looking out of the side window.

Starts were by Ki-Gas priming, a hand-turned booster coil and a manual swing of the propeller, a hazardous procedure which, on one occasion led to an engine backfire and a conflagration. Capt. Pascoe leapt out of the cockpit with an extinguisher and had the fire out before the awful realisation came to him that the poor old girl was worth more dead than alive! After 1947 the C. of A. was not renewed and the Courier was eventually burnt.

A Courier took part in a very interesting experiment in 1936, taking what were, perhaps, the first faltering steps in relay satellite technology. The Baird Television company wished to check the range of the picture transmitter at Crystal Palace; as VHF signals are "visual" and interrupted by high ground, the only way was to install a receiving set in an aeroplane.

Basil Clarke, the aviation writer, was one of the research engineers at Baird and was a member of the Baird flying club. He was responsible for ground tests in several types of aeroplane, all of which failed due to excessive interference from the ignition system. Clarke recalled a conversation with K.L.M. who found, quite by chance, that their Fokker airliners with engines fitted with Townend ring cowlings permitted very long range radio reception on high frequency, due it seemed, to the screening effect of the cowlings.

Baird could not afford to charter a Fokker, but the Courier appeared to meet the requirements. They chartered one from Hanworth and carried out an entirely successful ground test. They fitted an aerial array which, as Mr Clarke said in a letter to the author, "Would have sent the Air Registration Board round the bend," and took off. The picture was clearly recognisable, if a little ragged round the edges. It was the first time that a television picture had been

The only post-war survivor of the Couriers, G-ACVF, which was flown by East Anglian Flying Services until 1947.

Aeroplane Monthly

Courier G-ACLT before take-off, left, and after Sir Alan Cobham had landed, forgetting to lower the undercarriage, below. Unshaken, Sir Alan announced a test to prove that the Courier suffered little damage in a wheels-up landing!

Opposite page: Courier G-ACVF, impressed in April, 1940, as X.9437, at No. 5 Maintenance Unit in 1944. The undercarriage is fixed. *The Aeroplane*

Left: The hi-jacked Courier G-ACVE which two employees tried to fly to Spain.

received in an aeroplane anywhere in the world. The tests indicated that the picture could have been received as far away as Paris.

When the Spanish Civil War broke out emissaries of both sides were busy buying almost anything that would fly with armament. Several Couriers had been ordered and fitted with long-range tanks, but the day before the delivery flights were scheduled the Foreign Office prohibited their despatch.

A few days later, at 8.30 a.m., a Courier taxied out for take-off, wallowed unsteadily into the air, stalled and crashed into a ditch near the aerodrome boundary. The two occupants, who were very badly injured, were a woodworker who had never flown before and a mechanic who had flown once as a passenger.

They had broken open the flight test hangar where the machines for Spain had been stored, managed to start the engine and take off, hoping to teach themselves to fly once they were in the air. They had spent the previous few days trying to learn how to read a compass by studying one in the stores.

The idea was to fly to the French coast, turn right and press on until they reached Spain, where they hoped to circumvent the machinations of the British Government, pick up a cheque and return in triumph to the factory. A classic example of the path to Hell being paved with good intentions.

The repercussions of this matter were far-reaching. Officialdom was convinced that Airspeed was behind it and posted a posse of police at the works before ten o'clock that morning. As one executive said, "There seemed to be a policeman at every bench!" One of the engineers obtained permission to taxi an aircraft over to the flight shed only on condition that two policemen accompanied him, one in the cabin and one at the tail. Unfortunately he taxied at about 40 m.p.h. and the external guard ended up lying hatless across the tailplane.

CHAPTER THREE

Envoy and Viceroy

AT the beginning of 1934 the ever-present financial problems had caused Tiltman and Norway to conclude that only a major injection of capital into the company would allow it to survive. By the end of February another extension to the factory had been negotiated with Portsmouth Corporation, at a time when the guaranteed overdraft had been exceeded by over £2,000.

Airspeed was being "noticed" by the City of London financial establishments. There was also a possibility that the Air Ministry would ask them to submit a proposal for a new fighter aircraft, but, as was so often the case in those days, honeyed words were a poor substitute for action. No more was heard of it.

A company associated with Swan Hunter and Wigham Richardson, the Tyneside shipbuilders, was already providing finance for aircraft under construction and they began to take an interest in Airspeed. Negotiations commenced. Swan Hunter's final proposals were acceptable to the directors and shareholders and the new company, Airspeed (1934) Limited, was formed with Lord Grimthorpe, Sir Alan Cobham, Leonard Tetley, N. S. Norway and Hessell Tiltman remaining as directors with three Swan Hunter nominees, Charles Sheritan Swan, Sir Philip Wigham Richardson and George Wigham Richardson. So, at last, financial stability was within reach, though not before time, as the salaries of the directors were already two months in arrears.

The *Daily Express* announced the takeover, the first in the history of the aircraft industry, in resounding prose. The headline read "Plans for Mauretania of the air, dawn of a new commercial era." The paper quoted Sir George Hunter, "While it was an idea, or an ideal, to build large aircraft on the Tyne no definite preparations had been made in that respect. They would concentrate on Portsmouth first."

The *Express* continued: "It will mean that the builders of the *Mauretania*, the Old Lady of the Atlantic, have turned their attention to the building of *Mauretanias* of the air. It is almost certain that thousands of idle men, whose only hope of employment now is the building of other 534s [the *Queen Mary*, lying idle at Clydebank], will soon be at work constructing flying hotels whose size will be beyond anything generally imagined now."

After the takeover one of Swan Hunter's senior production men, Alfred Townsley, was asked if he would consider an assignment to Portsmouth for six months to sort out the production problems. He accepted and moved South; all

50

his friends in the shipyard thought he was completely mad to jump into such a hot seat in such a chancy industry, but he went ahead, spent the rest of his working life with Airspeed and made an immense contribution to its success.

At the end of 1933 the interest aroused by the Courier among small airlines and charter operators, themselves very short of cash, had led Hessell Tiltman to consider the next design, which he thought should be a twin-engined machine based on the Courier and using as many common parts as possible. Experience with the Napier-engined Courier suggested that the new Napier Javelin engine would suit the new design, to be numbered A.S.6 and later to be named Envoy.

Possible alternatives were the recently announced de Havilland Gipsy Six air-cooled in-line engine and the Wolseley A.R.9 radial. It soon became apparent that the Napier unit had no chance of competing with the Gipsy Six in world markets as de Havilland already had a well established service network at home and overseas. Airspeed could not take the risk of being dependent upon a powerful competitor for its engines, so the Wolseley engine, with the backing of Morris Motors in the field, was decided upon. The Armstrong Siddeley Cheetah was a possibility for a high-performance version of the Envoy if it was required.

Norway and Hessell Tiltman discussed the design with various operators who were interested in re-equipping. Almost without exception they demanded

The Envoy prototype, minus port engine cowling, contrasts with contemporary R.A.F. aircraft, Furies and Virginias, at Portsmouth in 1935. *The News, Portsmouth*

Envoy fuselages under construction in the Portsmouth works.   *Airspeed Limited*

a higher performance than the Wolseley engines would give. As was so often the case with the small and inexperienced operator, high speed was very attractive, the magic 200 m.p.h. (322 km/hr) was the optimum until the economics of the faster machine were revealed. Thereafter the Wolseley-powered version was most acceptable.

The announcement of the MacRobertson Race to Australia had prompted the entry of four Couriers. Squadron Leader Brady, of Aircraft Exchange and Mart, Airspeed's U.K. distributors, introduced T. Neville Stack, a well-known sporting pilot, who wished to compete if he could arrange suitable sponsorship. He hoped that one of the sponsors would be Lady Houston, whose philanthropy to aviation in the 'Thirties was legendary. Stack had ambitious ideas and wanted an A.S.6 with Rolls-Royce Kestrel engines. The price of £12,000-£15,000 shook him considerably, and he was finally content to accept a Cheetah-engined machine with a cruising speed of 180 m.p.h. (290 km/hr) and a duration of six hours.

The Board had discussed the new project and its market potential in November 1933. Stack's enthusiasm led Sir Alan Cobham to express his interest in a Cheetah-engined entry for the Australia race, and Lord Grimthorpe, the chairman, wished to associate himself with this entry, so, with two firm orders in prospect, the decision was made to produce the A.S.6.

Amy Johnson, a shareholder in the company, wrote to say that she was looking for a very fast single-seat, single-engine machine with a cruising speed of

200 m.p.h. (322 km/hr), a range of 4,000 miles (6,440 km) and a service ceiling of 30,000 feet (9,100m). Airspeed had no capacity to quote for this project but were flattered by the galaxy of star pilots who approached them for such thoroughbred aeroplanes. It was seen as a tribute to the publicity received by the Courier and its "Retractor" undercarriage.

So Tiltman proceeded with the detail design of the Envoy. He finally decided to follow the same basic construction as with the Courier, which had proved to be easy to build, strong and very reliable. The airframe was wholly of wooden construction, the fuselage being a semi-monocoque structure in two sections, the front fuselage, comprising the cockpit, cabin, toilet and luggage compartment, and the rear fuselage, carrying the tail unit. The doors and windows were built integrally with the sides and the stressed ply skin cut away before assembly. Distortion was avoided and the doors fitted perfectly. All the major fuselage sections were jig built with longerons of spruce and a skin of birch ply laid at an angle of 45 degrees. No diagonal bracing was needed as the skin carried all the shear loads, bending loads being carried by the longitudinal members.

The fuselage shell comprised two sides, a bottom and a top panel, to form a light, rigid box. The top and bottom curvature was formed with formers and stringers covered in fabric.

The Envoy prototype flying over the Cunarder *Queen Mary* as she sails down Southampton Water in 1934.   *Airspeed Limited*

The Series 1 and 2 Envoys had a twin-spar wing with Warren girder inter-spar bracing, the leading edge covered by 1mm ply, and the wing was fabric covered. It was stiff in torsion and was complicated to build. Moreover, as speeds increased fabric covering became less attractive. The Series 3 Envoy, introduced at the end of 1936, was built with a ply-covered wing, the two spars forming a torsion box to eliminate the Warren girder bracing and give a stronger and stiffer wing. The production time for the wing was reduced by 35-40%. The tail unit was a wooden structure, fabric covered.

Series 1 aircraft were designed without flaps. Pilots unaccustomed to the landing characteristics of very clean monoplanes complained that the Envoy just floated across the aerodrome and would not touch down, and to overcome this

The pilot's cabin of the Envoy.
Flight

criticism hydraulically operated split trailing edge flaps were installed in Series 2 and 3 aircraft. These extended from aileron to aileron and effected a considerable reduction in landing speed with a steeper gliding angle. With flaps down the stalling speed was reduced by 11 m.p.h. (17.7 km/hr).

The undercarriage was geometrically and functionally similar to the Courier and operated by a hydraulic handpump. Airspeed became involved in a legal battle over this undercarriage with de Havilland, claiming that they had infringed, in their Comet racer, Airspeed's retractable undercarriage patent. It was said that the action was a "friendly one" to establish a principle. *The Aeroplane* primly recorded its regret at "its good friends de Havilland and Airspeed being involved in legal argument and putting into the pockets of lawyers money which would help British aviation more if it was spent on advertising in *The Aeroplane*."

In parallel with the design work on the Envoy, Tiltman was also working on the Cheetah-engined machine, for Stack. This required so many variations from the basic Envoy that it was decided to identify it as the A.S.8, to be known as Viceroy.

A batch of six machines was laid down. The initial flight test of the prototype, G-ACMT, was scheduled for April 1934. Maximum effort was made to meet the dead line, but modifications to the airframe and the complexity of building with different engines caused much delay. In traditional fashion the Works blamed the Drawing Office and the D.O. blamed the Works. Tiltman, in his diary, praised them both very highly and revealed that most of the delay was caused by argument with the Air Ministry over wing strength factors.

At Farnborough deep prejudice existed over cantilever wings and R.A.E. demanded a 25% increase in the load factor. This would have played havoc with

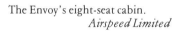
The Envoy's eight-seat cabin.
Airspeed Limited

the economics of the Envoy. Ultimately, after four months of negotiation, Tiltman convinced the boffins that such an increase was quite unnecessary, although, to prove it, a complete wing was tested to destruction. It was the first time that such a structural test had been carried out in this country.

On 26th June, Flight Lieutenant C. H. S. Colman flew G-ACMT for the first time. It handled extremely well with no snags and was demonstrated at the Society of British Aircraft Constructors Show at Hendon on 2nd July. The impact of this elegant aeroplane among the rather primitive Service types on display was startling. Most were dated biplanes, none was faster than the Envoy and all had fixed undercarriages.

The Certification trials at Martlesham Heath were beset with troubles, mainly with the Wolseley engines in which two fuel pump spindles sheared. A failed gasket in the hydraulic system caused the machine to land with one undercarriage leg half down, with consequent damage and delay. The fuel tanks developed leaks which were not easy to rectify. The major problem, however, was that the machine was overweight and its single engine performance was not satisfactory. It was felt that the new Wolseley IB engines would cure this defect. Generally the test pilots were extremely impressed with the overall handling and performance of the Envoy and a Certificate of Airworthiness was issued on 9th October 1934.

Stack's Viceroy was becoming a major worry, as all entries in the Australia race had to be handed over to the Royal Aero Club scrutineers by 14th October. Airspeed were to be well represented. Lord Nuffield, the founder and chairman of Morris Motors, and Lady Cobham had both entered Envoys, Sir Alan Cobham, Aircraft Exchange and Mart and R. K. Dundas entered Couriers, and all required modification in one form or another. The manufacturers of the Viceroy's engines and automatic pilot failed to keep their delivery promises and the machine did not fly until 19th September.

To add to Airspeed's problems the engine revs were low and the weight high. The Envoy's Cheetah VI engines of 315 h.p. each gave it a top speed of 210 m.p.h. (338 km/hr) at 7,000 feet (2,135m). It cruised at 190 m.p.h. (306 km/hr) and, with a massive long-range fuel tank in the cabin, had a range of 1,400 miles (2,253 km).

To save time, a Martlesham test pilot flew to Portsmouth to carry out the C. of A. trials. The machine was completely satisfactory, with a top speed of 210 m.p.h. (338 km/hr).

The race was in two sections, absolute speed and handicap with a maximum elapsed time. The Viceroy was so heavily handicapped as to have virtually no chance. It was the scratch aircraft giving 35 minutes to the specially designed DH. 88 Comet racing aircraft, one of which won.

To succeed in the handicapped section the Viceroy would have to average over 180 m.p.h. (290 km/hr), a sheer impossibility for a machine with a maximum cruising speed of 190 m.p.h. (306 km/hr).

As the scratch entry, Stack and his co-pilot S. L. Turner had arranged to take to Australia films of the start of the race. Only one other Airspeed aeroplane left Mildenhall on 19th October. This was Sir Alan Cobham's Courier G-ACVF flown by the 50-year-old Squadron Leader D. E. Stodart, with his young cousin as co-pilot. All the other Airspeed entries were withdrawn for various reasons. Stodart arrived in Melbourne on 29th October after a hair-raising ordeal in storms over the shark-infested Timor Sea. The Courier was sixth to finish and fourth on handicap.

Stack's Viceroy was forced down at Abbeville in Northern France with electrical trouble. The weather was foul, and although he soon took off again for Marseilles he had to return almost immediately. During the evening of 20th October he left for Rome, reached Athens and withdrew from the race. At the end of 1935 Stack and Turner sued Airspeed for "the recission of a hire purchase agreement and repayment of £2,448 paid by them for the Viceroy." They

Neville Stack's A.S.8 Viceroy with its Cheetah VI engines, which was scratch aircraft in the Mildenhall-Australia air race of 1934. *Flight*

alleged that Airspeed had been negligent in failing to ensure that the aircraft was fully airworthy.

The case was settled out of court, the plaintiffs withdrawing all their allegations and agreeing to return the Viceroy to the company with a further payment of £1,850. It was an unfortunate contretemps which benefited only the legal profession.

The same year, 1934, also saw the tragic end of Envoy VH-UXY, originally to have been built for R. K. Dundas as a demonstrator for India. At an early stage in construction a cable was received from the famous Australian airman Charles Ulm, who had been associated with Sir Charles Kingsford Smith and had flown with him on a number of his record-breaking flights in the Fokker tri-motor *Southern Cross*. He wanted to shorten the time from San Francisco to Sydney by using an aircraft from Honolulu to Sydney and ship for the difficult and dangerous leg from San Francisco to Honolulu, a distance of 2,200 nautical miles. He intended to survey the whole route by air, and if he was satisfied with its feasibility he would raise sufficient capital to operate airliners with the range to do the island hops across the Pacific.

He ordered an Envoy by cable and insisted that it should be filled to capacity with fuel and a crew of three. The maximum permissible weight would allow fuel for over 3,000 miles (4,830 km). This would require a large tank in the cabin, over the centre of gravity.

Ulm and his co-pilot G. M. Littlejohn arrived at Portsmouth to supervise the final preparations five weeks before the machine was to be shipped. Ulm was dynamic and impetuous and both men were very popular at Portsmouth, Tiltman finding Ulm most knowledgeable and extraordinarily thorough. His directness caused great hilarity in the shops. When he saw the toilet arrangements that had been installed in the Envoy he roared "You can take that bloody thing out at once!'' When asked how he proposed to manage without it he replied ''Simple! just use the bloody windows!''

One of his decisions caused serious misgivings. The tank in the cabin left a very cramped area forward for the two pilots and the navigator, with his equipment and chart table. Ulm decided that the navigator should move into the cabin aft of the tank where Ulm himself could not check any of the calculations.

The short time allowed to complete the aeroplane necessitated day-and-night working in the factory, with weekend work for the D.O. As the machine was heavily overloaded to 9,200 lb (4,140 kg) special wheels were ordered. When they were delivered they were found to be too small in diameter.

Three days before the delivery date for shipment three broken mainplane ribs were discovered. Tiltman played for safety. He assumed that the overload was responsible, stripped both wings and reinforced all ribs which were vulnerable. The Envoy was flying again within 40 hours. An automatic pilot and a fuel jettison valve were also installed.

So Ulm, Littlejohn and VH-UXY sailed for Canada in the freighter *Ascania* whilst Airspeed returned to normality, with Tiltman well satisfied with the aeroplane. On 3rd December Ulm, Littlejohn and their navigator, J. L. Skilling,

Ulm's Envoy VH-UXY being loaded on board the liner *Ascania*.   *Aeroplane Monthly*

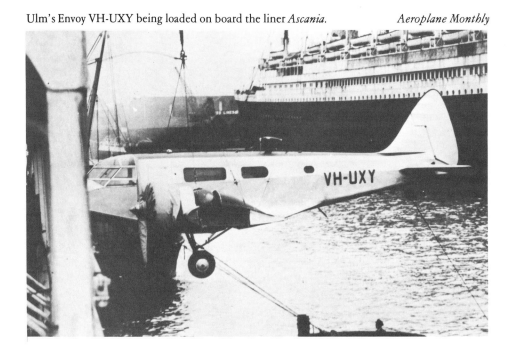

took off from Oakland, San Francisco, at 11.43 p.m. GMT. At 6 a.m. on 4th December they radioed their position 910 nautical miles south-west of San Francisco and had increased speed from 130 to 150 m.p.h. Ulm said lightheartedly that "The boys are getting hungry and have started operating on chicken sandwiches. The motors are working smoothly and we haven't got our feet wet yet." Later, Ulm gave their position as 400 nautical miles from Honolulu and reported to the liner *President Coolidge* that the weather was favourable and everything OK.

At 7 p.m. listeners were alarmed to hear "We do not know whether we are north or south of the islands. Weather bad, altitude 12,000 feet." At 7.15 "Very little petrol left, need a beacon urgently but do not want to send out an SOS so tell them to snap it up."

Whilst the tragedy inexorably developed, the Honolulu radio station was frantically trying to help them by sending continuous signals. It was assumed that their transmitter was working but not the receiver. At 11.20 came the call "We are south of Honolulu but are heading back on course now." At 11.25, "Off course again in heavy cloud and strong winds. Petrol only for 15 min., can planes stand by?" 11.30, "Coming down, just hitting the water."

At 11.58 came a strange message, "I have landed on the water and am now turning the machine into wind. Come and pick us up. I believe we can keep afloat for two days."

Nothing more was heard or seen of men or machine, in spite of a massive air-sea search carried out by thirty U.S. Army and Navy aircraft, nine submarines, three minelayers, two Coastguard cutters and many small craft from cabin cruisers to sampans.

The following day the London *Daily Express* headline announced that the liner *President Coolidge* had found them 374 miles from Honolulu. Sadly it was a mistake. For several days the seas over a 300-mile radius of Honolulu were combed, yet not even a piece of wreckage was found.

The disaster was a great shock to Airspeed, who immediately concluded that the navigational error which caused it was compounded by Ulm's decision to isolate the navigator in the rear of the cabin. The American Press published severe criticism of the workmanship of the Envoy which had been reported by mechanics at Oakland.

Hessell Tiltman was asked to make a report to the Directorate of Civil Aviation. He stated that the aircraft was in the air for 20 hours 15 minutes. If it had been flown in accordance with the theoretical optimum conditions recommended by Airspeed at 138 m.p.h. (222 km/hr) cruising speed, the range would have been 3,400 miles (5,474 km) and duration 24.7 hours. At 150 m.p.h. (241 km) the range would be reduced to 3,100 miles (4,990 km) and a duration of 20.7 hours.

A speed of 150 m.p.h. at 5,000 feet (1,524m) would have reduced the range to 2,700 miles (4,347 km) and the duration to 18 hours. Since Ulm's radio reports referred to both 150 m.p.h. (241 km/hr) and 12,000 feet a duration of 20 hours from take-off to descent into the sea was not unreasonable.

The most likely explanation of the crash was that the Envoy had a following wind which the navigator did not recognise. Their Honolulu landfall was scheduled for dawn. They probably flew right over the island in darkness and bad weather and were in fact flying further away from their destination. Skilling was a very experienced Orient Line navigator but had no experience of air navigation. His location in the rear of the cabin ensured that the very experienced Ulm could not check his charts or radio log. So they perished.

In his diary Tiltman recorded a comment which will strike a chord with all engineers who have experience of "specials". "I think the company should now have learned a definite lesson that these special racing or long-distance record machines are not a reasonable proposition. The relatively small advantages of possible success are more than balanced by damage experienced due to failure. Also they never pay since these special aircraft are always fabulously expensive." It is ironic that force of circumstances ensured that Airspeed continued to build "specials" until the Oxford trainer flew in 1937.

In 1934 Anthony Fokker, the famous Dutch designer and manufacturer, had acquired the European manufacturing rights for the new Douglas DC.2 airliner. He, in turn, sold sub-licences to manufacturers in a number of European countries.

Fokker's aeroplanes had been the scourge of the Royal Flying Corps in the First World War. On his return to peacetime activities he had built a range of very attractive and efficient airliners which were in service with K.L.M.

He had a memorable theory that aeroplane designers of all nations got away with things that no motor-boat designer ever could, simply because the spray from a boat can be seen. As no spray could be seen from an aeroplane, it was not possible to appreciate how badly designed the shape of it was. He asked what would be thought of a motor-boat designer who, when he wanted to increase his power, put a couple of extra engines on outriggers on each side.

Having evolved this theory, his major preoccupation was "cleaning up". On his return from the United States, where he studied the Douglas in detail, he said that he was ashamed to have his name associated with the aeroplanes that bore it. He had taken the trouble to clean up the general outline of his machines and to cut off obvious outgrowths which threw out spray, but in the DC.2 the designers had studied every detail. They had won half a mile an hour by cleaning up one thing, another mile or so by smoothing off something else and gone over the whole design in a wind tunnel and finally in flight.

"And so," he said, "you get half a mile here and a mile there, you add them up and then the World says 'What! 40 m.p.h. added speed all of a sudden! this is impossible!'" Fokker said that Donald Douglas realised that better performance could be obtained more easily by brain power than by more fuel.

He said that, as a hard-headed Dutch businessman, it made sense to acquire the licence. It cost £70,000 to develop the DC.2, and, even if he had the £70,000, it would still take at least two years of experimental work to achieve the same result. What he had bought was not only the know-how of an aeroplane to fly fast on limited power but the knowledge of how to make it at a reasonable price. Tooling up was not unduly expensive, because every component was designed for cheap production.

One of the Swan Hunter directors, disillusioned by the methods of the aircraft industry, so different from the solid Victorian approach of shipbuilders,

A Douglas DC.2 at Croydon in 1936. This aircraft, a forerunner of the famous Dakota, had considerable influence on aircraft design, not least in the Airspeed drawing office.
Aeroplane Monthly

introduced Tiltman and Norway to this remarkable Dutchman, no doubt thinking that he would be a most valuable ally in offering an independent view of these strange goings-on at Portsmouth.

Swan Hunter could not understand the mentality of these apparently frivolous aeronautical engineers. Hessell Tiltman told the story of a conversation with one of their directors who said "Tiltman, I cannot understand why you need thirty-five draughtsmen to design these tiny aeroplanes, we designed the *Mauretania* with far less!" Tiltman was slightly nonplussed by this comment, and sadly he did not recall his answer.

Tiltman and Norway were impressed, as Fokker shared their own philosophy of aerodynamic refinement and had the same compulsion towards economic production. Tiltman took a cautious view, however, realising that the financial implications of producing the DC.2 at Portsmouth were most alarming and that for a one-time enemy alien to be privy to the Board Room and Design Office secrets of Airspeed could ruin their chances of obtaining military orders.

George Wigham Richardson and Norway flew between St Moritz,

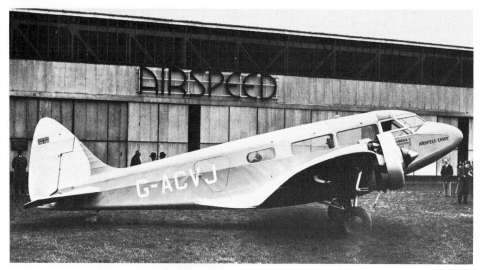

Envoy G-ACVJ, built for R. K. Dundas as a demonstrator for India, outside the Airspeed works at Portsmouth.   *Flight*

Flight Lieutenant H. C. Johnson and Sir Alan Cobham about to leave for India in G-ACVJ, January, 1935.   *Flight*

Newcastle and London during the autumn and winter of 1934. Fokker was an extremely difficult man to find as he appeared to have no settled home, and Norway recalled one occasion when negotiations commenced in an empty restaurant at three in the afternoon. Sullen waiters served lunch for the two Airspeed directors whilst Fokker drank a glass of milk.

In January, 1935, Norway, Tiltman, Flight Lieutenant Colman and a pilot named Ayres flew a Courier to Gravesend to meet Fokker, who was flying in from Amsterdam to demonstrate a DC.2 to Imperial Airways. They left Portsmouth in fine weather but ran into very rough air near Sevenoaks with cloud down to 100 feet (30m). A few miles from Gravesend the decision was made not to risk a landing, as the weather had become much worse. However, as they flew away the cloud drove them even lower and a forced landing was essential if they were to avoid the risk of flying into high ground.

Ayres quickly spotted a field which seemed suitable and put the Courier down. It was a soft harrowed surface and the machine tipped on to its nose as it came to rest. Fortunately the only damage was a bent propeller. They were extremely fortunate. When they ultimately reached Gravesend Airport they found that Fokker had flown the DC.2 to Gatwick.

Fokker's demands for his services seemed to Tiltman to be quite outrageous. He wanted a down payment of £20,000, an additional £20,000 when the turnover reached £100,000 and 1% commission on turnover. Additionally he was to have £50,000 of shares in the company. This meant that in five years they would have to pay him between £50,000 and £60,000, in addition to which he could make £50,000 on his shares. Hessell Tiltman recorded in his diary that "this is very big money for technical advice and everything depends on how conscientiously Fokker kept to his part of the bargain." He felt that Airspeed would never build the DC.2 but would prepare a special design embodying the principles of Douglas and Fokker.

So the agreement was signed and Fokker was consultant to the company for seven years. There were grandiose plans for building giant flying boats on Tyneside, but they came to naught; no airlines wanted such machines, and the fact that Swan Hunter had built magnificent ocean liners did not induce Imperial Airways and other operators to beat on their doors with orders for leviathans of the air.

In the spring of 1935 an enquiry was received from the Greek Government for fighter aircraft. The Fokker D.17 suited them but, for currency reasons, they could not buy from Holland. It seemed logical that Airspeed should build them under Fokker's guidance. Norway spent three frustrating weeks in Athens with a Fokker representative and achieved precisely nothing. He came to the conclusion that the Greeks were impossible people to deal with and flew home. His experiences formed the background of his very successful novel *Ruined City*.

Alfred Townsley, the general manager who had joined Airspeed from Swan Hunter, told how, soon after his appointment, Norway began to come to his office at the end of the day and engage him in conversation about shipbuilding and the problems of the yards. This pattern continued for several months and then ceased. Some time later Norway came into the office with a book.

"Townsley, you might like to read my new novel." So Townsley read it, and found to his astonishment why Norway had spent so much time with him. He went to Norway's office and said "Look here Norway, this is downright immoral, you have picked my brains for your wretched book, what do I get out of it?" Norway laughed. "I have just sold the film rights for £10,000, so I will give you a ticket to see it when it is shown in Pompey."

The Fokker adventure achieved very little for Airspeed. A major flaw in the drafting of the agreement was the failure to restrict payments to Fokker to earnings made from aircraft of Fokker design. So, ironically, Fokker benefited from the success of the Oxford, a machine which was designed quite independently of the Dutchman.

One project which may have been influenced by Fokker was the A.S.14 Ambassador. This machine was a high wing monoplane of mixed construction with two Bristol Pegasus radial engines and accommodation for 12-15 passengers, of which a cabin mock-up was built and a large scale model shown at the S.B.A.C. Show at Hatfield in 1936. No airline showed any interest, however, and with the development of the Oxford moving into high gear no further work was done on this design.

Lord Ronaldshay, who was mainly concerned with overseas sales, had suggested to Hessell Tiltman that R. K. Dundas could be interested in an Envoy with the Armstrong Siddeley Lynx engines for overseas service, where the extra power of the Lynx would compensate at "hot and high" aerodromes. Tiltman originally rejected the proposal on the grounds that the extra weight of the engines and fuel would adversely affect the payload and increase the landing speed to an unacceptably high figure.

The technical success of Ulm's aircraft, which received a Certificate of Airworthiness at an all-up weight of 5,850 lb (2,654 kg), a substantial overload, induced the designer to review the proposal. He concluded that the overall performance of Ulm's machine was better than the theoretical calculations had indicated. It was decided to build a demonstrator, G-ACVJ, for R. K. Dundas with Lynx IVc engines of 240 h.p. each. It was test flown by Flight Lieutenant Stainforth, who commented most favourably upon its performance and handling characteristics. It was fast, free from vibration, and had excellent take-off qualities. It was demonstrated to Imperial Airways and Railway Air Services, but neither airline showed any interest.

Fitted out as a six-seater with a large luggage or mail compartment, G-ACVJ left Portsmouth in January 1935, flown by Flight Lieutenant H. C. Johnson and Sir Alan Cobham, en route for India. Sir Alan had previously flown it to Spain for a demonstration to the Spanish Air Force, who showed interest in a military conversion carrying guns and bombs and powered by Hispano Suiza radial engines of 330 h.p. This project was stillborn, although the demonstrator, in common with a number of other Envoys, was sold to Spain in 1936, after the outbreak of the Civil War. Among them was G-ACMT, the prototype, whose career ended in a crash into high ground, carrying to their deaths Franco's General Mola and the crew.

As a postscript to Tiltman's diary entry on the Lynx Envoy he plaintively records "We are, as usual, having a lot of enquiries for this machine fitted with every engine but the one we have fitted to it."

64

The Envoy entered airline service in April 1935, with North Eastern Airlines. The company was formed by Lord Grimthorpe to open up air routes between London, Leeds, Newcastle and Glasgow using the Cheetah-engined machines, G-ADAZ *Tynedale*, G-ADBB *Wharfedale* and G-ADBZ *Swaledale*. The south-bound inaugural flight, carrying a party of civic dignitaries, came to grief at Heston when it overshot on landing and ran into the boundary fence. Fortunately nobody was injured and damage to the aircraft was superficial.

In May, *Swaledale* was in trouble with carburettor icing near Ripon, a belly landing being made in a field. Fred Slingsby, the famous sailplane builder and a competitor of Airspeed in their earlier days at York, who had his factory at Kirkbymoorside, was asked by Norway if he could salvage the Envoy to avoid the expense of sending a party from Portsmouth. Slingsby recalled the fury and indignation of the farmer who berated the very shaken pilot for having the temerity to land in his field of growing corn!

The fare from London to Edinburgh was only £10, but there was insufficient demand. The service terminated in July.

In the same year Cobham planned a service along the south coast and down to the Channel Islands using Envoys, G-ADAZ and G-ADBA.

Despite the failure of this service, Portsmouth, Southsea and Isle of Wight Aviation, of which he had become chairman, planned a service to Paris. New Envoys were ordered with Lynx engines, Marconi AD41/42 radio, Sperry artificial horizons, directional gyros and Reid and Sigrist turn and bank indicators, a very sophisticated specification for those days when civil aviation was largely ''flying by Bradshaw'', following the railway lines.

North Eastern Airlines' Envoy G-ADAZ *Tynedale* after it had overshot at Heston on its inaugural south-bound flight.   *Flight*

From 22nd July a daily service was operated from Portsmouth to Paris, 202 miles each way at an average speed of 135 m.p.h. (217 km/hr) in 90 minutes. The single fare was £4 15s. (£4.75) and £8 10s. (£8.50) return. The aeroplane was loaded to maintain flight on one engine if necessary and carried a crew of two, four passengers and baggage. Passengers pronounced the flight to be pleasant and not very noisy in the comfortable, well-ventilated cabin with its large windows. The Envoy had the same power and payload as its companion in the P.S.&IoW. fleet, the tri-motor Westland Wessex, but was 50% faster.

An Envoy Series 2 sold to the Czechoslovak State Airline in 1935.   *Aeroplane Monthly*

The Czechoslovak airline C.S.A. ordered two Series 2 aircraft, OK-BAL and OK-BAM fitted with Czech Walter Castor engines. Two Czech officials who visited the works to place the order were most insistent upon a firm delivery promise and included a penalty clause in the contract. When the Czech party appeared in London at the end of July 1935, to take delivery of the first machine, R. D. King, the Sales Manager, was a very worried man. Completion was, in fact, five days late.

Fate, and the medical profession, played right into his hands. Several of the Czechs were quite exhausted after their long and gruelling journey by rail and sea and wished to be taken straight to their hotel. King was most solicitous and convinced the most weary gentleman of the party that he should see the company doctor. The company doctor was well briefed and confirmed King's diagnosis that they were most certainly in no fit state to fly an unfamiliar aeroplane back to Czechoslovakia, so they relaxed for a few days, and then left in OK-BAL, marvelling at the consideration shown to them by the executives of Airspeed.

Two further Envoys were ordered by C.S.A. in the following year, Series 2

Karel Brabenec, the millionaire chief pilot of C.S.A., and chief WT operator B. Soukup with Envoy OK-BAL at Portsmouth.   *Airspeed Limited*

OK-BAN and OK-BAO. Series 3, OK-VIT was delivered to the Czechoslovakian Iron and Steel Corporation, for the use of the Managing Director.

The C.S.A. aircraft opened a service from Prague to Moscow. On the proving flight OK-BAL flew in four stages a distance of 1,430 miles (2,300 km), averaging 148 m.p.h. (238 km/hr.), and landing in the dark when necessary, using only its own landing lights. The machine aroused great interest among the Soviet pilots and engineers at refuelling points, accustomed as they were to the rather crude Russian aircraft.

The scheduled service began on 1st October. It was the longest airline service in Europe, taking 9 hours 40 minutes, including stops. An extension to Bucharest and Uzhorod was planned. Reliability in the extremes of cold and heat was so remarkable that C.S.A. planned further extensions to Brussels in conjunction with SABENA and to Venice with Ala Littora. In the first month of operation the two Envoys flew 7,460 miles (12,000 km) without trouble; the State airline expressed complete satisfaction.

The Envoy was displayed at all the European air shows, often being the sole British participant. It was announced in August 1935, that Japan Air Transport had decided to order Envoys instead of Fokker Super Universals; the machines would ultimately be built under licence at the Mitsubishi Works at Nagoya.

Two six-passenger Series 1 Envoys had already been despatched to Japan and two eight-passenger Series 1s ordered. Altogether 11 Envoys were built in Japan between 1936 and 1938. It was intended to instal Japanese engines, which were fitted in the prototype, but this aircraft crashed on a test flight, killing the pilot. It was considered that the larger diameter engines had created an airflow problem in the centre section area and induced a premature stall. Future machines were fitted with two Lynx.

The Envoys operated scheduled services between Tokyo, Osaka and Fukuoka. Some were sold to Manchuria Air Transport for service in Manchuria and Korea, but little is known of their operation.

The arrival of 1936 saw the Envoy well established with charter companies and small airlines, whilst Cyril Colman flew a busy programme of demonstration flights and air shows, with a few races for good measure.

Early in the year Airspeed had commenced production of a batch of Special

The Envoy prototype converted to Series 2 standard with flaps in 1936. *The Aeroplane*

The Envoy prototype G-ACMT with an experimental four-blade propeller installation.

The Aeroplane

Series 2 machines for the South African Government, this type becoming known as the Convertible Envoy. Only ten man hours of work effected transformation from a luxurious airliner to a fairly lethal warplane. *The Aeroplane* commented in July "but even thus stripped, the Envoy still provides its crew of three with interior decoration and soundproofing by Rumbold so that they can go into action in armchair comfort."

Hitherto the South African Air Force had been equipped with Junkers aircraft, and the Airspeed order caused some controversy in South Africa. Many people thought that more Junkers machines should be bought, so Airspeed and British aviation were on trial.

The tests of the Convertible Envoy at Portsmouth and Martlesham Heath were very encouraging. With Cheetah IX engines, the machine in its civil guise reached 208 m.p.h. (333 km/hr) in level flight, was perfectly steady in a dive at 300 m.p.h. (483 km/hr) and climbed to 10,000 feet (3,000m). As *The Aeroplane* said "The designer, in his original sin, takes advantage of the increase in wing loading . . . to use bigger motors and so get increased performance."

The wing loading was 18.6 lb/sq.ft. (9.1 kg/sq m). The flaps, standard on Series 2 aircraft, enabled low landing speeds to be achieved in spite of what was, in the 'Thirties, a rather high wing loading.

Driven on by their ambition to lead, Norway and Tiltman evaluated different propellers, from fixed-pitch wooden ones to the new variable-pitch

One of the Series 3 Convertible Envoys built for the South African Air Force in 1936. *Flight*

units which, in 1935, were considered to be expensive luxuries. They flew a pair of Smith propellers on an Aries-engined Envoy, but decided that the potential market did not justify the expense involved, and finally settled for the Fairey-Reed fixed-pitch propeller, a slab of duralumin twisted and machined to give a very thin and efficient blade section.

With the exception of two special Oxford prototypes and the A.S.45 Cambridge trainer prototype in 1941, no Airspeed machine was fitted with V.P. propellers until the Ambassador airliner in 1947. Variable-pitch propellers were, however, specified for a number of projects not built.

Seven Convertible Envoys were ordered. Four were to be used by South African Airways and the three military versions by the South African Air Force.

On 4th July 1936, a civil and a military machine, ZS-AGA and No. 251, left Portsmouth for the 7,000-mile (11,260 km) flight to Johannesburg. The civil aircraft was flown by Capt. Elliott Wilson of the S.A.A.F., accompanied by George Errington, an Airspeed test pilot, and ground engineer Scott. No. 251 was flown by Capt. Donnelly and W/O Whittaker of the S.A.A.F.

In these days of Concorde and Jumbo jets, one tends to forget the hazardous nature of long-distance flying in the 'Thirties. Navigational aids were rare and rudimentary, and ground support facilities limited and usually difficult to organise in advance. In the *Airspeed Bulletin* of Autumn 1936, George Errington gave a diverting account of the delivery flights of these two Envoys.

70

They flew to Cologne, Frankfurt and Vienna in foul weather, and on to Budapest, Belgrade, Salonica and Athens. From Cairo they flew at low altitude over the Valley of the Kings and landed at Luxor among Arabs who had a distinct sense of humour, in addition to distinct scents. One had a very doubtful firearm, and the direction in which he held the spout was a matter of minor consideration to him. Leaving a covey of Arabs, including the gentleman with the gun, guarding the machine, they were transported into town over a rather amazing road in an equally amazing car, the hood of which regularly collapsed upon the passengers.

They left Luxor for Khartoum, over the Blue Nile, down the White Nile and around a very violent thunderstorm. Malakal was the first aerodrome they encountered with a runway. A night stop at Juba enabled the "poor bloody ground engineer" to survey his new surroundings whilst extracting oil filters and examining tyres, propellers and the airframe. Occasionally a batch of coal-black and very skinny Mammies passed along in single file, performing incredible balancing feats with the day's shopping on their heads and accompanied by even skinnier husbands who carried long spears, "presumably for prodding the missus," said George Errington.

From Khartoum ZS-AGA flew to Nairobi via Kisumu to pick up Mr Pirow, the South African Prime Minister, who was flying on to Pretoria. Mr Pirow was the first to greet the crew on the tarmac. He and his party were impressed with the report of the flight given to them by the South African pilot; 5,000 miles (8,000 km) had been flown in 30½ hours in great comfort without any problems. George Errington waited at Nairobi for No. 251, delayed at Cairo by the R.A.F., who showed great interest in the Envoy.

Four days later, Errington boarded Donnelly's No. 251 and flew to Pretoria via Dodoma and Mbeya, where they noticed seemingly endless miles of scrub with bush fires raging in all directions. George concluded his account of the flights with a handsome tribute to the Shell Company's organisation, which had 87-octane fuel waiting for them even hundreds of miles from railways, whilst the four Armstrong Siddeley Cheetah engines behaved beautifully, giving never a moment's anxiety.

The other five Envoys had been delivered by sea. Errington supervised their assembly at Wynberg Air Station, Capetown, carried out flight tests and trained the South African pilots. The first machine to arrive by sea came to grief in the hands of a South African Air Force pilot, Lieutenant Bates. The starboard undercarriage leg retracted on landing as the oleo leg took the weight. Other than a bent propeller, a shock loaded engine and a damaged wing tip, little damage was done. The fault was attributed to damp in electrical circuits.

One of the aircraft was totally destroyed in June 1938, killing the crew of two and the four members of the Royal Air Force boxing team visiting South Africa. The Envoy was flying near the Rhodesia/Bechuanaland border when it was believed to have collided in cloud with a huge vulture, wreckage and bodies being spread over a wide area of wild bush land. The circumstances were particularly horrifying as the bodies of the victims were badly mauled by wild animals.

Victor Burnett, the Air Correspondent of the *Sunday Express*, on a flying holiday in South Africa, offered his services in the search for survivors. A two-page article on June 12 described the dangers encountered by the ground parties trying to penetrate the dense bush, constantly harried by lions and hyenas. It was described as a "Hoodoo Operation"; everything went wrong. Vehicles broke down and crashed; the engines of the aircraft which was to carry the coffins home would not start, and when these were transferred to another

Handley-Page H.P.42 Hengist of Imperial Airways at Croydon. These biplanes were so slow it was said that all Imperial's profits were made in the bar on the flight between Croydon and Paris.

Flight

machine this could not be started either; and to add to their problems the rescuers were menaced by a rogue elephant. The tragedy stirred the sympathy of the South African people and a substantial sum was raised by public subscription for the dependants.

Once again Airspeed's market appreciation proved to be over optimistic and the print of 1,000 Convertible Envoy sales brochures was largely wasted. No more machines were sold. Nevertheless, the splendid service which the seven Envoys gave in South Africa paved the way for the 500 Oxfords which went to South Africa and Rhodesia during the Second World War.

At least two of the Convertible Envoys saw war service, though their ultimate fate is unknown.

An Envoy caused a crisis at Croydon and questions in the House of Commons. Air Dispatch Limited had developed a regular and extremely reliable newspaper and freight service to Paris. The first flight left Croydon at 5 a.m. loaded with newspapers and other urgent freight, returning with freight and bullion and making further trips as the market demanded. At 10 a.m. a service called "The Blue Plane" left with passengers who could transact their business in Paris and return in good time for dinner. On this flight a hostess was carried.

Air Dispatch were meticulous in keeping to schedule with their three Envoys, and often their advanced navigational aids ensured that they were the only machines to get through in marginal weather. This caused a little jealousy with certain officials of Imperial Airways who were operating Handley Page H.P.42 Hannibals, venerable assemblies of aircraft components which were so stately and slow that some said that all Imperial's profits were made in the bar on the way across.

The pilot of one of the sleek Envoys forgot to lower his undercarriage before landing at night and caused a major obstruction. Having no adequate lifting gear, Air Dispatch appealed to "Big Brother", who first agreed to help and then withdrew the offer. The ensuing row reached the Commons, the Honourable Members being treated to a diatribe by Mr O. E. Simmonds, M.P., who accused Imperial Airways of "Wanting all unsubsidised airlines left out in the cold."

It would appear that even in those halcyon days no love was lost between the national carriers and the independents.

On 21st July Air Dispatch's G-ADAZ, bought from Cobham, flying the newspaper run to Paris and Madrid, stopped at Le Bourget and Biarritz dropping off papers and collecting three journalists who were to be the first to cover the Spanish Civil War at first hand. The pilot, Roland Falk, stayed for three days at Barajos, Madrid, still in Communist hands. He saw the manager of the hotel and a guide shot dead.

Falk's departure on 25th July was delayed by the harassing tactics of Customs. With four passengers and three crew, the only way of escape was to brandish a file of completely irrelevant documents before the scruffy and illiterate officials. The ruse worked and they took off, hotly pursued by a rebel aircraft. They blessed the Envoy's performance as they reached the Pyrenees at full throttle. Their relief was short lived, however, as an exhaust valve failed in the port engine right over the mountains. Fortunately they were able to maintain sufficient height on one engine to reach Biarritz, where a rough landing broke the tail wheel post. There they remained for several days until a new part could be flown from Portsmouth. This flight was the first visit by a British aircraft to Madrid since the Civil War broke out.

Falk reported that 600 British citizens were clamouring to be evacuated. A small fortune could have been made in bringing them out if Air Dispatch had not been so heavily committed with the newspaper contract.

A major event in the sporting flying calendar for Autumn, 1936, was the Portsmouth to Johannesburg race for the Schlesinger Trophy and cash prizes. The Airspeed Viceroy bought by Neville Stack for the MacRobertson Race and returned after the lawsuit had been sold to Max Findlay and Ken Waller, two very experienced sporting pilots, who received an extremely good offer from Spain and the Viceroy was used in the Civil War. Findlay then ordered a standard

Ken Waller and Max Findlay with their Envoy G-AENA before the Portsmouth-Johannesburg race.
Flight

Max Findlay's ill-fated Envoy *Gabrielle* with the race number 13 on the rudder. *Flight* ▶

Cheetah-engined Series 2 Envoy with long-range tanks and radio equipment.

Registered G-AENA and named *Gabrielle*, it bore the racing number 13 on the rudder, a fact which drew comment from the superstitious when it was wheeled out of the paint shop at Portsmouth.

Concord Morton, who handled Airspeed's publicity, recalled an eve-of-race dinner party with the crew of G-AENA and C. G. Grey, editor of *The Aeroplane*. The table gradually filled up until Grey pointed out that there were 13 people around it.

The race itself was thought to be a fiasco; of nine starters only one finished. Findlay and Waller, with A. H. Morgan as radio operator and C. D. Peachey as engineer, were first to leave Portsmouth and made good progress to Cairo. Between Cairo and Khartoum they made a navigational error and landed at Kerma, 80 miles (129km) off course, when fuel shortage caused one engine to stop. They found some very dubious Government petrol and were delayed for two hours trying to start the engines on this witches' brew. Power was right down and the take-off was hair raising.

After a push start by natives, the Envoy bumped and bucketed across the pot-holed track and clawed its way into the air after a run of one mile (1.6km). By this time, unknown to the crew, half the petrol had evaporated in the terrific heat and one engine failed near another village, where they landed to refuel with motor spirit.

Soft sand resulted in another terrifying take-off, and they just reached Khartoum as one of the main tanks ran empty. Imperial Airways engineers spent 8½ hours checking the aircraft and reported that the magneto switch on the

starboard engine was shorting out the magneto, but nothing could be done to rectify it. They had trouble with this engine all the way down to Abercorn, where yet another refuelling stop was called for. The carburettor enrichment control on the Envoy comprised one lever for both engines, and they were continually juggling with it, to the detriment of the port engine, to keep the starboard one running.

At Abercorn they learned that Scott and Guthrie, the ultimate winners, were a few hours ahead of them and there was a fighting chance that they could catch them. Abercorn was not a regular route stop but merely a scrubland strip originally cleared for Sir Alan Cobham 11 years previously, with surrounding trees lopped to a suitable height to give a run of 1,000 yards (915m) east to west and 650 yards (590m) north to south. The altitude of the strip was 5,500 feet (1,676m) above sea level, with a gradient downhill eastward, so to take off into wind the Envoy had to travel uphill. Local officials tried unsuccessfully to dissuade Findlay from loading extra fuel drums in the cabin and to persuade him to wait until sundown when the wind would die down.

The pilots were in a frantic state and spurned all advice; with Findlay at the controls the machine taxied at high speed to the down end of the strip, quickly turned and, with engines at full throttle, moved with agonising slowness over the rough ground. When they reached the middle of the strip, Mr Young, the resident Shell representative, who was watching with Mr Glennie, the District Commissioner, shouted "They'll never get off." As they approached the boundary he said "They're finished."

To the astonishment of the onlookers the machine took off at the last moment and slowly rose to a height of 30 feet (9m), flying satisfactorily but very slowly. A short distance from the boundary the Envoy lost height, the starboard wing tip struck a tree and lost four feet of the wing. It banked to the right due to the loss of lift and the broken wing struck another tree, tearing off the whole of the wing outboard of the nacelle, the machine rolling into the ground and totally disintegrating. Findlay and Morgan were found just ahead of the wreckage, dead. Waller was nearby, practically uninjured, and Peachey was unscathed in what remained of the rear fuselage.

Norway and Tiltman were very upset by this crash, which was surrounded in mystery. It was not clear whether there was a defect in the aeroplane or whether pilot error was the cause. In any case, apart from the loss of life the publicity surrounding the accident in an international race was not relished by Airspeed.

Norway despatched George Errington, whose skill as a pilot had quickly been recognised by Cyril Colman when George joined Airspeed as an approved inspector in September 1934, to Abercorn to report at first hand on the circumstances of the crash. Educated at Uppingham and Sheffield University, where he took an engineering course, George had spent several years in the design office of Vickers Limited, moving to A. V. Roe at Manchester in 1929. He took a course in aeronautical engineering, obtained Ground Engineer Licences A and B, and joined the Comper Company at Hooton in 1932 as an approved

Refuelling *Gabrielle* at Portsmouth for the Johannesburg race. *The Aeroplane*

inspector. He bought an Avro Avian which he maintained himself and then acquired a Comper Swift, which he rebuilt after a crash had severely damaged both airframe and engine. He completed his collection of Ground Engineers Licences and flew the Comper all over Europe and Scandinavia. It was still flying in the 1960s as G-ACTF.

George's mission to Abercorn made the headlines in the *Sunday Express* when he chartered a de Havilland Puss Moth and managed to lose himself in the bush for two days. The vibration of the Puss Moth upset his compass and the mainspring of his watch broke, so direction and elapsed time were unknown. In low cloud he flew over Abercorn, finding himself low on fuel over swamp, scrub

A de Havilland Puss Moth similar to that chartered by George Errington for the flight to Abercorn.
Aeroplane Monthly

and hills. He saw a native village which had, as he discovered later, the only area of flat ground for miles around, and made a good landing, missing, miraculously, many ant hills. When he left the machine to reconnoitre he was assailed by the ants and hastily returned to the Puss, which was being watched by terrified natives who had never before seen an aeroplane and thought it a great bird which had come out of the sky to destroy them. By sign language George was able to persuade the Chief to send a runner to the nearest white official.

After a night spent in the Puss Moth listening to violent thunder storms, Errington welcomed the District Commissioner who arrived with tins of fuel. The natives honoured him with a festival dance and cleared a track for take-off, which at an altitude of 6,700 feet (2,044m) was distinctly hazardous. He flew on to Abercorn to inspect the wreckage, blissfully unconscious of the sensational stories headlined in the national dailies, "Famous Test Pilot lost in Jungle", etc.

His report on the crash was a model of logical deduction and this narrative is based upon it. He explained the loss of height which caused the impact with the first tree as the result of Findlay taking off with a little flap down, realising as they climbed that the flaps would cause drag and making the fatal error of selecting flaps up before a safe height had been reached.

Evidently Norway commented upon the extravagance of chartering the Puss Moth as, at the end of the report, he explained that the alternative was a flight by Imperial Airways to M'Pika at a cost of £52 return and a hire car to Abercorn, 480 miles (773km) with petrol at 3s. 6d. (£0.18) per gallon. The cost of hiring the Puss was £62 18s. (£62.90) which George thought appeared to compare favourably. Norway evidently concurred, as nothing more was said.

The organisers of the Schlesinger race generously donated the £6,000 prize money left, as only one entrant finished, to the wives of Max Findlay and A. M. Morgan and to Findlay's daughter for her education.

The October issue of the *Airspeed Bulletin* recorded that a luxuriously equipped Scorpio-engined Series 2 Envoy, VT-AHR, had been delivered to His Highness the Maharajah of Jaipur by his personal pilot, Mr J. Stewart Hill. The seating caused considerable interest at the time, being designed to adapt quite automatically to the posture of the occupant. 'HR gave good service in India until it crashed in 1942.

Airspeed's experience with the Wolseley engines had convinced them that these units were certainly the right ones for the Envoy and they were designing the new Oxford trainer to be powered by them. Serious difficulties had arisen between Lord Nuffield, Wolseley's chairman, and the Air Ministry. Nuffield was not accustomed to the costing methods embodied in the "Instruction to Proceed" system set up as part of a cost control exercise for re-armament contracts. Having already invested £200,000 in the aero engine business, he felt that large-scale production of engines for the Ministry with no fixed price contract could bring the motor-car side of his business to ruin as well as the engine plant. On 14th October 1936, it was announced that Wolseley's were terminating the production of aero engines.

This was a most serious blow to Airspeed, with an order for 150 Scorpio-engined Oxfords pending. Norway decided to visit Nuffield to try to persuade him to give Airspeed the aero engine business for nothing. In *Slide Rule* he describes the meeting: "Nuffield was still furious with the Air Ministry. He grew red in the face at the thought of them and thumped the desk before him. 'I tell you, Norway, I sent that I.T.P. thing back to them and I told them that they could put it where the monkey put the nuts!'."

So a good engine was lost to the nation through bureaucratic arrogance.

Besides being Coronation Year in Britain, 1937 was a vintage year for Airspeed's overseas marketing activity. Orders for two Envoys were received from the Governor of the State of Kwangsi for the personal use of His Excellency and his staff. The first aircraft, G-AERT, was delivered by Flight Lieutenant C. H. A. Colman in January to Luikhow Airport, with Mrs N. S. Norway as a passenger and an Airspeed Technical College student, W. F. Locke, later to become managing director of an Airspeed subsidiary company, Fireproof Tanks Limited, as the ground engineer.

G-AERT met bad weather and flooded aerodromes from Portsmouth to Athens, and yet from Marseilles to Pisa, where bad visibility necessitated a

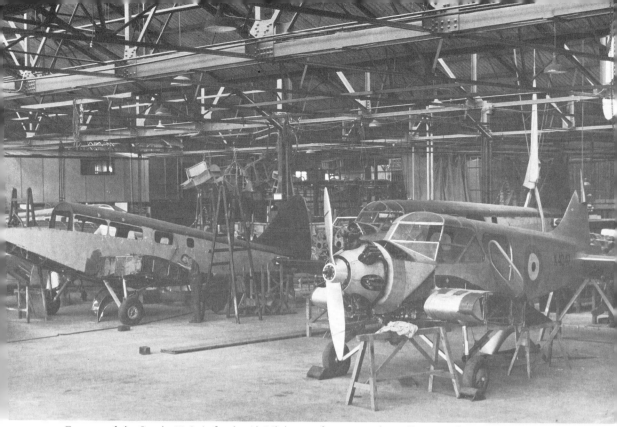

Envoys and the Courier K.4047 for the Air Ministry under construction at Portsmouth.

The Aeroplane

landing, the Envoy averaged 185 m.p.h. (298 km/hr). Through Persia to India over the most varied country, the pilot experienced all the vagaries of the weather.

The Envoy landed at Delhi, where the crew was welcomed by Lord Ronaldshay, chairman of R. K. Dundas Limited, Airspeed agents in India. They flew via Allahabad, Calcutta, Rangoon and Bangkok to Hanoi in Indo-China. En route to Hanoi a forced landing was necessary at Lakhon, an emergency landing ground in Siam on the border with Indo-China. Here crowds surrounded the Envoy, laughing and shouting and trying to reduce the aeroplane to pieces as souvenirs. Unfortunately, none could speak English so, to repel the marauders, Colman decided to frighten them by starting the engines as if to take off again. Shortage of fuel and the fearful weather conditions called his bluff, so he taxied the Envoy to a hangar where, in the midst of much confusion and difficulty, he managed to preserve it. Two hours later the hangar was emptied of visitors and two French residents had arrived to introduce the crew to the local Shell staff at Thahkek in Indo-China.

The French were particularly helpful and entertained them to dinner. This necessitated a trip across the river in a very unstable native canoe with a strong tendency to roll.

They returned in darkness and had great difficulty in locating the aerodrome and the Envoy. Eventually two very tired crew members spent a rather uncomfortable night in the machine. The weather cleared next day and they left for an uneventful flight to Liu-Chow.

At the headquarters of the Kwangsi Air Force hospitality abounded, and the party was introduced to the genuine Chinese chow and the technique of handling it with chopsticks. Colman gave the Chinese pilots a conversion course on the Envoy and flew the Military Governor to and from the capital, Kwei-lin.

The Governor's bodyguard of two heavily armed soldiers caused Colman, who hated fireworks, some anguish. On the first flight he noticed that from their belts hung grenades, supported by the rings used to withdraw the firing pin! Suitable alternative arrangements were hurriedly made.

It was said that Cyril Colman reduced the negotiations to the simple formula "You no bloody bombs or me no bloody fly!" This was clearly understood.

The Chinese authorities were so pleased with the Envoy that Colman was instructed to send a cable to Portsmouth and order another one to be delivered as quickly as possible.

This one, G-AEXE, left Portsmouth on 15th June piloted by G. B. S. Errington, accompanied by another student, R. M . Graham,. This flight was a remarkable achievement on the part of George Errington, who had made his first flight for the company in 1935.

The two delivery flights to China were probably the longest of their kind ever attempted, and in *The Aeroplane* of 6th October 1937, Errington wrote:

> "Our flight took twelve easy days and 53 hours flying time from beginning to end. Apart from the monsoon area from Calcutta to Bangkok, there was little fatigue in the flight, a fact which speaks very well for the aeroplane, the tireless running of the motors speaks well for them, too. The Chinese were distinctly pleased with the speedy delivery of their aeroplane, we were received kindly and hospitably, and, although we never fully mastered the chopstick technique, I have the pleasantest recollections of Kwangsi Province."

Before returning to Portsmouth he flight tested a new fighter built in the Province.

An interesting coincidence provides a link with the delivery to the Chinese National Airline in 1978 of the last of 36 Trident airliners, which were designed by de Havilland. One of the test pilots mainly concerned with the testing and delivery of these aeroplanes was Ron Clear, who had been an Airspeed test pilot from the late 'Thirties and worked with George Errington until George was killed in the Trident deep stall crash near Norwich in 1966.

An export order in 1937 for a Series 3 Envoy F-ABBQ was from Ste Air Pyrénéés who were to develop a service between Toulouse, Biarritz and Bilbao. Delivered on 20th March, it made 55 flights in 39 days before coming to an untimely end before the guns of Spanish Nationalist fighters, as M. Galy, the pilot, reported:

"About six and a half miles (10 km) from the landing ground I was attacked by five Nationalist fighter aeroplanes. After the first attack I thought they had made a mistake and turned to enable them to get a better view of my French registration and the inscription Air Pyrénéés shown on the fuselage. I had hardly begun to turn when four other aeroplanes which were near began to fire, and, without stopping, all five aeroplanes riddled me with bullets.

"After the first burst of fire I lost one blade of the port airscrew and had to stop the engine immediately. Then another burst of fire tore away half the port aileron, blocking the control wheel completely in a position giving a list to port. After that the aeroplane had no further lateral control and I thought the end had come. All the same I tried to save the lives of my five passengers, whatever the cost. I cut the starboard engine, lowered my flaps, leaving the undercarriage up, this latter to avoid turning over in such uneven country. At the moment of touching the ground I pulled the stick towards me as hard as I could. The machine fell from about ten feet (3m) and stayed where it had fallen. The shock was such that the fuselage was broken in two, thus making an emergency exit for my passengers.

"Personally I had a few cuts on the face, but my passengers all came through the accident unhurt. I am certain that it is thanks to the robust construction of my Envoy, and particularly to its wood construction, that we owe our lives." He could have added for good measure, a high standard of airmanship and incredible luck.

The ultimate accolade for Airspeed came when an order was received for a Series 3 Envoy for the King's Flight to be used for the transport of Royalty and V.I.P.s. This magnificent machine, G-AEXX, was painted in the colours of the Household Cavalry, red, royal blue and silver. The interior was styled by Rumbold and it was, indeed fit for a King. Four passengers were accommodated in great luxury and a steward occupied the rear of the cabin.

In *Slide Rule* Norway commented upon the requirement for a steward in an aeroplane where the passengers were likely to be aboard for only an hour or two. Wing Commander E. H. "Mouse" Fielden, the Captain of the King's Flight, explained to him the utter fatigue which the Royal Family endure when on a major visit, opening Town Halls and shaking a thousand hands. Norway said no more about the need for a steward.

Rather naturally, all the senior staff wished to be involved with the Royal Envoy. Fielden was not amused and delivered an edict that if the order was to be placed he would deal with two people only, Norway and R. W. Cantello, who was in charge of the Experimental Department and had responsibility for G-AEXX.

Cantello recalled the occasion when the image of the aeroplane was somewhat debased after an undercarriage failure at Renfrew. He had a frantic phone call from Jenkins, the ground engineer, informing him of the failure and the fact that they had to fly Prince George to the West Country the next day. There was no time for new parts to be flown to Scotland, but a hurried search of derelict airport buildings had revealed an old iron bedstead. This was dismantled to provide a jury strut which was lashed to the defective radius rod so that they could fly to Portsmouth for nine o'clock next morning. Cantello had a shrewd idea of the parts required and had these ready.

His secretary, a most meticulous young lady, had for many months tried to persuade the company to replace her very ancient typewriter. At last agreement was reached that she should have a new Underwood typewriter, which she insisted upon. At 9.30 a.m. she answered the telephone to learn that the "Royal machine had arrived". She was furious, saying very forcibly that she had ordered an Underwood, not a Royal. However, the misunderstanding was cleared up, the aircraft repaired and the Prince's schedule remained undisturbed.

Crank-starting the port engine of an Envoy belonging to Portsmouth, Southsea and Isle of Wight Aviation in 1935.
Airspeed Limited

Lord Grimthorpe arranged for the Envoys in North Eastern Airways to have a plaque installed at the front of the cabin informing the passengers that the aeroplane was identical with the one in which the King flew.

On the outbreak of war 'XX was "called up" and, as L7270, served with No. 24 Communications Squadron throughout the war. It was again registered as G-AEXX after the war, ultimately being sold to a Swedish owner to be registered SE-ASN. It was one of the few Envoys to fly after the war, another being G-AHAC, which had also seen service as an R.A.F. communications machine.

In 1938 the British Government gave 96 Blenheim bombers to the Indian Government to strengthen the Air Force out there. The Commander-in-Chief was Air Marshal Sir Philip Joubert de la Ferté, who inherited some elderly Avro aircraft as communications hacks. He bent one himself whilst flying it to Singapore, and decided that the occurrence could form the basis for the re-equipment of the communications flight.

After much wangling and persuasion the Air Ministry ordered two Envoys, G-AFJD and G-AFJE, later to be N9107 and N9108. Sir Philip was in the U.K. when the first was due to be delivered and decided to fly it to India.

He insisted that Service and Government officials at his stops en route should be told of the informal nature of the flight and that no ceremonial was called for. He was assured that only Service personnel would receive him, so the party flew in civilian clothes.

On arrival in Paris they were shocked to find a crowd of sightseers at Le Bourget and a full Guard of Honour with band. Sir Philip had to inspect the Guard wearing his oldest oil-stained flannel trousers. A similar welcome awaited

The Royal Envoy G-AEXX in its livery of red, royal blue and silver.   *The Aeroplane*

Envoy G-ACVI being built in 1934. In the background is the Air Ministry's Courier K.4047.

The Aeroplane

them at Lyons, where he was soaked inspecting a woebegone guard which had paraded in a thunderstorm. Thereafter, his wishes were observed.

Unfortunately the flight was plagued with technical troubles which caused anxious moments flying across the Anatolian Plains of Turkey, with the Taunus Mountains ahead and one engine on low power. They arrived safely at Karachi, where the Air Marshal briefed the Senior NCO at the depot, telling him that if he valued his career that Envoy must be absolutely right! Thereafter the two Envoys gave very good service in India.

In September the *Daily Express* caused great hilarity in flying circles by reporting a forced landing by Roland Falk en route to Doncaster in an Envoy. His undercarriage was jammed in the 'Up' position and a belly landing was inevitable. As repair facilities were available at Croydon he decided to return.

The *Express* said that "He knew he faced the risk of a fatal crash if he tried to land. An airport official said that they had made all preparations, an accident seemed almost inevitable, ambulances and the fire brigade were ready . . . everyone dreaded what might happen but Mr Falk handled the machine magnificently. After he circled round he zoomed to gain altitude. Then he shut off his engines, stalled, put the machine in a steep dive, flattened out just above the ground and made a perfect landing."

It was not, of course, revealed that the wheels of the Envoy project below the engine cowling when in the retracted position, so that such a landing could be made without serious damage. The aeroplane was flying again within two weeks.

So came the Second World War. The history of many of the 82 Envoys built has been lost in the mists of that conflict, but it is known that one of them, G-ACVI, first registered in the name of Lord Nuffield on 6th October 1934, was bought by Ansett Airways in Australia in August 1936. In 1944 it was re-engined with 350 h.p. Wright Whirlwind engines and by 1945 had flown over 10,000 hours. Its ultimate fate is not known.

The Envoy was undoubtedly a very fine aeroplane, aerodynamically advanced for its day with a beauty of line which reflected great credit on that consummate artist Hessell Tiltman. Even today an Envoy at Heathrow would stand comparison with the best of modern twins.

Essentially it provided the background for what was probably the finest twin-engine trainer in the world, the Airspeed Oxford, of which 8,586 were built.

The failure of Airspeed to make profit from its two outstanding airliners, Courier and Envoy, poses the question "Why?" This must be considered in the context of the economic and social circumstances of the 'Thirties, and the activity of the major competitor, de Havilland, with the DH.84 Dragon and DH.89 Dragon Rapide.

Both the Courier and the Envoy offered speed, but the internal routes were too short to show advantage, particularly as the railways offered a fairly fast, comfortable journey from city centre to city centre, relatively unaffected by adverse weather. So the businessman had little incentive to fly.

The Ferry was completely out of the running as soon as de Havilland built the Dragon, whose payload was 40% greater than the Courier's. Even the Envoy could not compete, in spite of its speed. In addition D.H. had a first-class servicing organisation throughout the world.

The Envoy was, however, successful overseas, where routes were long enough and traffic density sufficient to take advantage of its high speed.

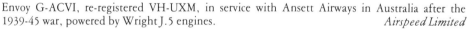

Envoy G-ACVI, re-registered VH-UXM, in service with Ansett Airways in Australia after the 1939-45 war, powered by Wright J.5 engines. *Airspeed Limited*

CHAPTER FOUR

Oxford

THE MID—Thirties were years of disillusionment. Perceptive observers of the European scene began to realise that the euphoria which followed the "War to end all Wars", as the 1914-18 conflict had been known, was a snare and a delusion.

In 1927, flagrantly contravening the terms of the Versailles Treaty, the Germans sent pilots in secrecy to Russia for military training. In 1934 Winston Churchill warned that the Royal Air Force, decimated after the war, was only half the size of the French Air Force and that Germany was re-arming at an alarming rate; indeed he expected them to achieve parity in the air within two or three years. In the Air Estimates of March 1934, a paltry increase of four squadrons of aircraft was proposed, a total of 40 machines costing £130,000.

In July a further proposal was made to increase the strength of the R.A.F. by 41 squadrons, but this was to be over a five-year period. Churchill expressed in eloquent terms his contempt for this pacifist Government dedicated to appeasement. Fortunately his oratory at this critical time alerted influential men, and the Government invited certain firms to submit private venture designs for consideration. So Sydney Camm designed the Hawker Hurricane, R. J. Mitchell the immortal Spitfire.

The Germans were developing the sleek Dornier Do 17, with a top speed of 290 m.p.h. (467 km/hr); our fastest fighter, the Gladiator, had a top speed of 255 m.p.h. (410 km/hr).

Slowly the defence dinosaur stirred, and specifications were issued for advanced aircraft which became the Whitley, Wellington, Hampden, Stirling, Halifax and Lancaster.

It was realised that training crews for these powerful and probably unforgiving aeroplanes would present problems. The Avro Anson coastal reconnaissance aircraft was considered for the role of trainer and was, indeed, widely used until the introduction of the Oxford at the end of 1937. "Faithful Annie" was far too much of a lady to be really satisfactory; a very undemanding aeroplane, it did not encourage the high standard of flying technique which would become vitally necessary when the much more unforgiving twins entered squadron service.

Airspeed were building a good reputation with the Air Ministry, but the Fokker link was handicapping them. All Government contractors were bound by the Official Secrets Act which prohibited any alien from entering the

One of the first batch of Oxfords to be delivered to
the Royal Air Force. *Flight*

THE FLYING INSTRUCTOR'S LAMENT

What did you do in the War, Daddy?
How did you help us to win?
Circuits and bumps and turns, Laddy,
And how to get out of a spin.

Well and alack and misery me,
And I trundle around in the sky;
Instead of machine gunning Nazis,
I am teaching young hopefuls to fly.
Thus is my service rewarded—
My years of experience paid.
Never a Hun have I followed down,
Nor ever gone out on a raid.

They don't even let us go crazy;
We have to be safe and sedate.
So its nix on inverted approaches—
They stir up the C.F.I.'s hate.
For its ever such a naughty example
And what will the A.O.C. think?

We never get posted to fighters—
We just get a spell on the Link.*

So it's circuits and bumps from morning to noon,
And instrument flying till tea.
Hold her off, give her bank, put her undercart down.
You're slipping—you're skidding—that's me!

And as soon as you're finished with one Course,
Like a flash up another one bobs,
And there's four more to show round the cockpit,
And four more to try out the knobs.

Sometimes we read in the papers
The deeds that old pupils have done.
And we're proud to have seen their beginnings
And shown them the way to the sun.

So if you find the money and turn out the planes
We'll give all we know to the men,
Till they cluster the sky with their triumphs
And burn out the beast from his den.

With acknowledgements to "WINGS", The Journal of the Royal Australian Air Force,
December 15th 1945.

*Link Trainer, a ground-based trainer.

Wren's cartoon of the Oxford, which was accompanied by the verse:

> In Oxford's many seats of
>   learning
> Sit the u/t air crew, yearning
> For that coveted, distant day
> When each in his particular
>   way
> Applies his Varsity education
> To accomplish Hitler's
>   decimation.

premises without Ministry sanction. The agreement with Fokker was beginning to go sour as it had achieved little but expense, so the Board used the Act to keep the Dutchman and his colleagues out of the Boardroom whilst continuing with half-hearted attempts to co-operate in the civil field. The association went slowly into decline as Fokker's health deteriorated. He died in 1939.

The Envoy had established a firm base for Airspeed. It was operating efficiently with airlines throughout the world and with a number of charter companies. One had come fourth in the Newcastle Air Race and won another race from Elmdon, Birmingham, to Yeadon, Leeds. Flight Lieutenant Colman had demonstrated it widely in Europe and its appearance at the Royal Air Force Display at Hendon had aroused considerable interest.

Because sales were low and unit costs consequently high, 1935 showed a very disappointing financial result. The *Investors' Chronicle* commented on 6th January 1936, upon Airspeed's first published accounts: "After allowing for depreciation a loss of £4,353 was shown after the transfer of an unstated sum to bad debts reserve. The chairman explained that profits had been earned when the interim dividend had been decided upon, but subsequently some customers had run into financial difficulties, cancelling orders and forcing the company to re-possess aeroplanes."

In this year Lord Grimthorpe decided that he must devote himself to his own activities and could no longer do justice to his position as chairman. Leonard Tetley, one of the original Airspeed directors, suggested George Wigham Richardson to replace him.

"Young George", as he was known, had taken immense trouble since he became a director to learn the background and detail of an unfamiliar industry; the Board agreed that he was an admirable choice. He held the office until de Havilland took over the company in 1940.

In December 1935, Mr Robinson of R.D.A.* 6 Civil at Air Ministry had

*Research and Development Air.

phoned Norway to enquire the price of a Lynx-engined Envoy. He was quoted £5,150. He then asked whether the type could be converted to a trainer, and if so, what would it cost? He was told that conversion was feasible and would cost £4,800 with the Wolseley Aries engine and £4,850 with the Scorpio.

By March 1936, the number of employees at Portsmouth had risen to 600 with an order book of £117,000. Although the international situation was so grave, the notorious Cabinet Minute restricting military orders to members of the S.B.A.C. and dating from the locust years of the industry was still being invoked behind the scenes to prevent Airspeed building first-line aircraft. Verbal assurances were given by officials that the factory would be kept busy for at least three years, and Tiltman was convinced that the Ministry would like to bring them into the privileged coterie of manufacturers but that the issue was too complex for a rational solution. He had heard from various sources that proposals for a new twin-engined trainer were being discussed and that, indeed, a quantity of 50 had been quoted. Tangible proof eluded him and he became more frustrated as the weeks passed.

In May an order was received for two prototypes of the radio-controlled target aircraft, the Queen Wasp, which will feature in the next chapter.

At last an invitation was received to tender for the new trainer to Specification T23/36, clearly written around the Envoy. For the first time the Ministry revealed their conviction that Airspeed was a serious contender for military orders for, admittedly, second-line types; the notorious Minute had been by-passed.

The Airspeed factory at Portsmouth in September, 1936.   *Flight*

An early production Oxford Mk.I, L.4576, on a test flight in May, 1938. *Aeroplane Monthly*

The Expansion Programme had certainly made it easier for them to obtain sub-contract work for a wide range of equipment, from pilot's seats to map cases. Such orders caused dislocation in the factory, planned for the production of complete aeroplanes. So many alterations to the plant layout and a disproportionate amount of tool room time affected the main business of the company, but it had the effect of showing the Ministry the production capability and versatility of the works and gave personnel valuable experience in the extension of techniques such as sheet metal fabrication.

Hessell Tiltman prepared and submitted provisional proposals for the A.S.10 trainer and negotiations with the Ministry dragged on interminably.

Alfred Townsley, the general manager, was rather disgusted with the offer of a contract for seven Oxfords for New Zealand as a "tooth cutting" exercise, which he realised would be totally uneconomic, so he arranged an appointment with the Air Minister himself. Lord Swinton saw the logic of his case and arranged an "Instruction to Proceed" for a further 50 aircraft. This, too, was inadequate for efficient quantity production, particularly as Townsley wished to set up what was virtually the first flow line production system in the aircraft industry based on Hessell Tiltman's new brainchild, photo-lofting.

Tiltman had visited the U.S.A. to study the technique of applying shipyard mould-loft practices to aircraft production. The Ministry of Aircraft Production placed contracts for the production of prototype etched aluminium plates in modules 6 feet × 4 feet. They were interchangeable throughout the industry, and layout tables could be bolted together in any size to allow the largest aircraft to be laid out photographically full scale. In a matter of months production times were reduced and a high degree of standardisation and interchangeability achieved.

This and the retractable undercarriage were among his greatest contributions to aviation.

Tiltman's diary entry for November 1936, was eloquent:

"Through months of grief and argueing which beggars description we negotiated the Contract. Many times it appeared to be quite hopeless. The programme now is for 136 machines and we have been advised to add from 20-25% extra for Colonial and foreign sales. Up to date the machine has had three changes of engine, the Scorpio and Cheetah being alternately decided upon. It now appears possible that a further change back to the Scorpio may be made. The aircraft, which will probably be called 'Oxford', has developed quite a long way from the original conception of a modified Envoy. It is now a 100% re-design, and the transition has been largely the cause of many of our troubles. D.T.D. (Directorate of Technical Development) realised from the start that nearly every feature would require changing but the production side of Air Ministry would not face it. By the end of 1936 30% of the design work had been completed in spite of the continual changes and disruption. The Ministry pretended to be

George Errington leaving an Oxford Mk.I after a test flight. *Aeroplane Monthly*

How the Airspeed Gazette saw ▶ the Oxford's first flight.

annoyed at the effect of all this upon the delivery programme but I imagine it is not as serious as they make out.''

Not the least of the problems was the uncertainty which surrounded the availability of the Wolseley engines. For weeks Lord Nuffield had negotiated with Whitehall and argued forcibly against what he saw as the unworkable Shadow Factory scheme. Ultimately, of course, he withdrew from the aero engine field shortly after an announcement had been made that his factories would build Army vehicles as well as aero engines.

Further battles with the Ministry produced an ''Instruction to Proceed'' for another 100 aircraft. This was quickly followed by a further Instruction for 250. So the Oxford was away to a flying start.

The Board quickly realised that they had not grasped the nettle of middle management problems which had held the company back. For too long the criterion of management ability had been willingness to invest money in the company. Townsley introduced H. W. Denny, a very experienced aircraft engineer, as works manager and great progress was made under his control.

The Oxford was of wooden stressed skin construction, the airframe being

divided into four sub-assemblies which could be built quite independently of each other, with minor finishing work after final assembly. The centre section, the major unit, extended to a point outboard of the engine nacelles and carried the mounting points for fuselage, engines and the undercarriage, which was hydraulically retracted rearwards. Mark I was to be a General Purpose Trainer, for all aircrew grades, with dorsal gun turret, bomb bay and ancillary equipment whilst Mark II was planned as a dual-control pilot trainer with no turret or bombing facilities. In practice the Oxford was used almost exclusively for pilot training and Mark I's usually flew without turrets. The engines were Cheetah IX's with wooden propellers.

Flight Lieutenant Cyril Colman flew the prototype, L 4534, for the first time on 19th June 1937, and was well satisfied with its performance. A week later it was shown in the New Types Park at the R.A.F. Display at Hendon. After this debut flight tests began in earnest under Colman and G. B. S. Errington.

George Errington had a hairy experience during the spinning trials of the type. These flights were to take place over Devon, and the effect on the spin characteristics of the machine was to be investigated at different positions of the centre of gravity with varying loads. With C.G. forward all was well, George allowed eight rotations and the recovery was simple, although the engine on the inside of the turn had a habit of failing. The spin was quite stable and the pilot was able to photograph the instrument panel on the way down, possibly another Airspeed "first" in flight test recording.

The technical department was satisfied after about 100 turns had been completed, and moved the load so that the C.G. was behind the aft limit. As these were the conditions which might cause difficulty, an anti-spin parachute was fitted at the tail, operated by a lever in the cockpit roof and released by a further lever alongside. As an added precaution George had a rope fitted along the centre of the fuselage to help him reach the door if it should be necessary to bale out with the aircraft in the spin.

So the nose of the trusty "Ox-box" was turned towards sunny Devon and a climb to 16,000 feet (4,876m) initiated. Errington checked his parachute and stopwatch and spun the machine with camera poised. After eight turns recovery action was taken. The machine ignored it completely. The time had come to deploy the tail parachute as only 8,000 feet (2,440m) was left before boring operations into the Devon soil commenced. The lever was pulled, but the Oxford ignored that too.

George decided to bale out smartly, released his harness and staggered aft to the door. Suddenly the spin ceased, the tail came up and a slow spiral dive developed.

George rushed back to the seat and pulled the parachute jettison lever, assuming that the 'chute had suddenly deployed. Again nothing happened.

Perhaps he hadn't pulled it hard enough. Another ferocious pull, as he said "Hard enough to shame a Scot at a fruit machine."

The whole lever assembly parted company with the cabin roof, complete with part of the roof, and swung around dangerously on its cables. By this time the distance to Devon was only 4,000 feet (1,220m) and shrouded in cloud for good measure. An immediate departure was vital, so again the pilot made for the door.

Again the machine began to recover, and again George rushed to the seat, with no time to do more than lean over the back of it to try to pull out of the dive as the altimeter unwound between one and two thousand feet, still in cloud. He tore out of cloud at high speed, missed a hill by 200 feet (61m) and flew straight and level with aeroplane and pilot trembling like jellies. Investigation proved that the parachute had deployed sideways and fouled in such a way as to jam everything.

Spinning was prohibited at Flying Training Schools; indeed the Service developed a mild phobia about it. Oxford Standing Instructions demanded that if the machine was still spinning at 5,000 feet (1,524m) the crew should bale out.

Cutaway drawing of the Oxford Mk.I.   *The Aeroplane*

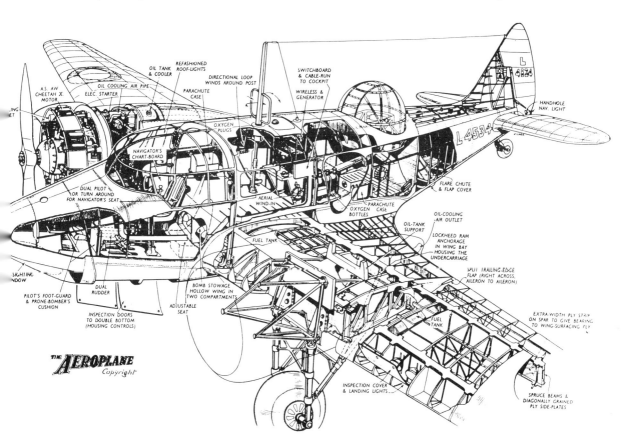

Some machines showed signs of heavy pre-stall buffeting, so R.A.E. Cranfield carried out a research programme on a production aircraft known to be a "rogue". It was found that the Oxford was particularly sensitive to misalignment between the engine cowlings and the wing root fillet. A leather seal was devised to close the gap, a distinct improvement on most aircraft.

In an attempt to find a universal cure a slat was designed to go over the wing between the fuselage and the nacelle. This was test flown and found to be the answer. Unfortunately it interfered with the hand starting crank and over-wing refuelling, so was not put into production.

Oxford N.6327 was converted to twin rudder layout to improve spin recovery characteristics, but surprisingly it made very little difference and the machine quickly reverted to its normal tail unit.

The Oxford was exactly right, and the modifications found necessary in the flight test programme were minor ones. The pitot head for the air speed indicator showed unacceptable position error and was moved from the aerial mast to the underside of the starboard wing. The mast itself was shortened and moved forward. Later the exhaust pipes were modified to accept a cabin heater muff, a modification which delighted pilots on winter nights. Service overseas led to the installation of Vokes air filters to the carburettor air intakes to avoid dust ingestion.

In addition to the twin rudder Oxford, there were a number of other experimental machines. The fifth production machine, L 4539, was modified by the Heston Aircraft Company to mount the Maclaren castering undercarriage.

The Oxford Mk. III with Cheetah XV engines and constant speed propellers. *de Havilland Aircraft*

Oxford N.6327 with twin rudders, designed to improve spin recovery characteristics.

Bruce Robertson

This was designed to compensate for drift in a crosswind landing, the aeroplane facing directly into the prevailing wind whilst travelling at an angle to it of as much as 30 degrees. It must have been a highly disconcerting experience for the pilot. The castering undercarriage was flight tested for over a year, but the problems of control on the ground and retraction of the undercarriage ruled out further development, and L 4539 was fitted with a standard undercarriage. Another machine, L 4538, was converted for British Airways, an amalgamation of Railway Air Services, Jersey Airways, and a couple of small charter companies, as a trainer for blind approach techniques and other radio navigation equipment.

In March 1940, the only Mk. III was built with Cheetah XV engines and Rotol constant speed propellers; the Mk IV was a projected pilot training version of the Mk III.

An oddity in the range was a Mk I, delivered to the de Havilland Engine Company and fitted with 250 h.p. Gipsy Queen IV engines purely for engine development purposes. The first photograph of this machine, issued in 1940, caused some consternation in high places when the left side of the photograph revealed the rudder and tailplane of the Mosquito prototype night fighter, at that time firmly on the secret list but overlooked by the censor. *The Aeroplane Spotter*, which first published the photograph, included an amusing caption by the cartoonist Chris Wren,

> ''Tales of old and tails of new
> creeping sternfirst into view,
> rest of body still concealed
> very soon to be revealed.''

A prototype Mk V was built with 450 h.p. Pratt and Whitney Wasp Junior seven-cylinder radial engines and Hamilton Standard constant speed propellers. This was the progenitor of the Oxford to be assembled in Canada for the Empire Air Training Scheme. Performance was extremely good and the ungeared engines conferred upon it the accolade of the noisiest British aeroplane in service.

W. F. "Bill" Shaylor, the commercial manager, had reported to a Design Committee meeting on 4th October 1938, that the Air Ministry were of the opinion that by June 1939, the requirements of the training programme of the R.A.F. would have been met and overseas sales would be permissible. Shaylor felt that they should negotiate to buy the prototype L 4534 for a nominal sum and approach Pratt & Whitney with a request that two of their engines should be loaned for test purposes. The Ministry demanded 90% of the original cost price, which, since the airframe was in poor condition, was quite unacceptable. So an entirely new aircraft was converted, years later.

Oxford Mk.I AS.504 fitted with a pair of Gipsy Queen IV engines.
Aeroplane Monthly

In the late 'Thirties and early 'Forties pilots were trained ab initio on de Havilland Tiger Moths, advanced training following on Miles Masters and the American radial-engined Harvard trainer. Bomber pilots were then diverted to the twin-engined Anson and, later, the Oxford.

This change from single to twin engines was a landmark in the career of a pilot. Hitherto he had been flying relatively simple aeroplanes, now he had to adapt to a machine which was radically different in several important characteristics, and the transition was almost as memorable as his first solo. The extra engine introduced a quite different mode of operation both in the air and on the ground. The pilot was no longer seated behind a long nose which gave a visual reference to the horizon and thus to his attitude. Taxiing references also changed considerably. His eye level was much higher, and he was no longer on the centre line of the aircraft. This, in turn, meant that in a side-by-side twin his engine controls were to his right hand in the centre console, not to his left. His aileron control was by wheel, not column as in the single-engine trainer. So a new sensory reaction had to be acquired.

In the case of the Oxford the changeover was greatly assisted by the superb layout of the controls and instruments. For its time, it was quite outstanding as the first British military aircraft to have a logically planned cockpit in which the controls required by both pilots were located so that they were easily accessible to each of them. Nevertheless, the Oxford was not an easy machine to fly and in this respect it simulated most accurately the "feel" of the bigger aircraft to which the pupil would soon graduate. It was accepted that at least 150 hours on Oxfords were necessary before the pilot could make it perform exactly as he wished. The machine demanded the precision which was the hallmark of the Royal Air Force.

Pilots' Notes referred optimistically to the Oxford "Exhibiting a slight swing to starboard on take-off". In practice it would gallop away to starboard if the throttles were not judiciously handled in conjunction with the rudder and brakes. It was necessary to straighten the tailwheel and lead with the starboard engine to full throttle; many a serpentine take-off path betrayed those who ignored this dictum and spectacular ground loops were not infrequent. Once speed built up a steady, light push on the column raised the tail, increasing visibility and rudder effect. At 70 m.p.h. (113 km/hr) a light pull would take the Oxford smoothly into the air; climbing at 110 m.p.h. (177 km/hr) would achieve the optimum rate of 960 feet per minute (293 m/min) at sea level.

The ailerons were light and well harmonised and the elevators powerful and easily trimmed. Surprisingly, the large rudder was not as effective as might be expected. The trimmer was inadequate, heavy and low geared, so single-engine flying was wearisome. The stall was straightforward at 67 m.p.h. (108 km/hr) on a good aeroplane and could be held against full elevator without a wing drop. Those machines susceptible to premature stalling of the wing roots showed even better lateral stability since the tips never reached the full stalled incidence. The minimum stalling speed was, however, increased significantly.

As the Service prohibited spinning in the Oxford, pupils' only experiences were inadvertent ones. Recovery could usually be achieved by normal procedures. Full throttle on the inside engine could sometimes assist recovery.

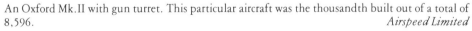

An Oxford Mk.II with gun turret. This particular aircraft was the thousandth built out of a total of 8,596. *Airspeed Limited*

The works management and flight team at Portsmouth.   *Airspeed Limited*

In the circuit the Oxford was a pleasant aeroplane with a good view and a comfortable speed of 120 m.p.h. (193 km/hr), which gave plenty of time to sort out "finals" on the downwind leg. Full flap pitched the nose well down, giving a good view, at 80 m.p.h. (129 km/hr) on a glide approach. A firm heave on the column would achieve what was usually a tail down "wheeler". Three-point landings were more demanding and were never to be recommended in a fair cross wind, because as the tail came down the rudder was blanketed and the deflected slipstream helix would send the Oxford charging off in all directions.

Overall it was a splendid aeroplane, a thoroughbred which would bite the careless or clumsy rider. A pilot skilled on the "Oxbox" could be expected to tackle any twin or multi-engine machine with a fair degree of confidence.

The first delivery to the R.A.F. took place in November 1937, when L 4535, 4536 and 4537 were delivered to the Central Flying School at Upavon for evaluation. R. E. Clear, later to become a test pilot with Airspeed, de Havilland, Hawker Siddeley and, latterly, British Aerospace, was charged with engineering support of these aeroplanes, which were being compared with the well-established Avro Anson. Ron Clear appreciated that reliability was of paramount importance but not easy to achieve with the first aircraft of a new type. He built up a fine rapport with the R.A.F. maintenance crews and, whenever a fault developed, a few bottles of beer, judiciously distributed, ensured overnight attention. If spares were required he would drive to Portsmouth to collect them, if necessary, from the production line.

Rumours of slight unserviceability occasionally reached the Chief Technical Officer, but all the Oxfords were on the flight line next morning. The type went on to build up a superb reputation for reliability in squadron service, quite independently of Mr Clear's machinations.

Ron Clear had left for Portsmouth early one morning when a senior

100

Airspeed man, R. W. Cantello, arrived to inspect the Oxfords in the hangar which they shared with sundry Hart trainers. Cantello was shocked to see a scene of devastation. One of the Oxfords was sprawled on its belly with the adjacent Harts, the wings of which overlapped the tips of the Oxford's wings, lying at a drunken angle, dragged over by the reclining aeroplane.

The affair was a mystery. Naturally everyone denied touching the cockpit retraction lever. On further investigation it was found that the Commanding Officer had brought his house guests and their children to the hangar to see the new trainer. It had to be concluded that inquisitive children were probably responsible. Fortunately little damage was done to the Oxford, and it was soon flying again whilst the Portsmouth design staff bit their pencils in an attempt to introduce suitable hydraulic safeguards.

Ron Clear was one whose appearance in the aviation firmament took place at an early age. *The Aeroplane* of 21st March 1934, comments: "We hear of a remarkable case of air enthusiasm. A boy named Ron Clear took his 'A' Licence on his 17th birthday on 8th February this year. He joined the Portsmouth and Southsea Gliding Club in 1930 at the age of 14, passed his flying tests after seven months during which time he had one accident caused by his light weight which allowed the glider to blow over on to its back whilst still on the ground.

Test pilot Ron Clear with a Trident airliner after a test flight. He followed George Errington's delivery flight of an Envoy to China in 1937 by delivering some of the thirty-six Tridents ordered by China's national airline in the 1970s. *Hawker Siddeley*

"He could not acquire his gliding certificate at the time because he was not seventeen . . . his case persuaded the Gliding Section of the Royal Aero Club to lower the age and he got his certificate in October 1931.

"In June 1933, after failing to kill himself on several home-made gliders, he came to the Wiltshire School of Flying at High Post as an apprentice. He got his Ground Engineer's Licence and went solo after 2½ hours dual in the club Moth. He did 3½ hours solo and obtained his Pilot's Licence on his seventeenth birthday.

"Young Mr. Clear lives at Portsmouth and rides up to High Post, 45 miles away, to his work on a motor bike in all weathers, covering 100 miles a day on a singularly uncomfortable conveyance."

Ron Clear retired from test flying in 1980 to become aerodrome manager for British Aerospace at Hatfield. Few test pilots can match his 49 years of flying.

Alfred Townsley explaining interchangeability jigs to Air Minister Sir Kingsley Wood. Centre background is Hessell Tiltman, left is Flight Lieutenant C. H. S. Colman and right is H. W. Denny.
Airspeed Limited

Airspeed were encouraged in the summer of 1937 by the visit of the Air Minister, Sir Kingsley Wood, in company with Air Marshal Sir Wilfrid Freeman, Sir Edward Campbell and Sir Charles Bruce-Gardner, chairman of the Society of British Aircraft Constructors. They saw Oxfords in production and inspected the new Queen Wasp target aircraft and the Royal Envoy G-AEXX, which was undergoing its Certificate of Airworthiness inspection. On the production line was an Envoy for the RAF.

Sir Kingsley, in a speech to the staff, praised Portsmouth for its contribution to the defence of the country and said of Airspeed: "This progressive firm has made and is making a considerable contribution to our aircraft production, which, I am glad to say, is steadily gathering momentum. There is one thing that I would like to say about this firm, and that is that since it first undertook work for the Air Ministry it has never let us down, that is about the highest praise that one could give to any firm today. As the country knows, we are considerably augmenting our sources of aircraft supply and this company is an example of an organisation which has received large direct contracts for aircraft entirely of its own design. They are doing well and there has, I am glad to say, not only been a steady increase in production but in labour recruitment as well.

"One of the secrets of the success of the firm is undoubtedly its good labour relations . . . there is real team spirit in the factory."

Assembling the cockpit canopy of an Oxford. *Flight*

This was no hollow public relations bromide, it was a fact, evident to all who visited Portsmouth. It prevailed until the gates closed for the last time in 1968.

Certainly there were problems. One of Airspeed's longest-serving men, George Twyman, a whimsical character, told the story of the occasion he interviewed a labourer who had refused to carry out an instruction to clean out the wood mill. The man was most aggressive. "Yer don't know, mate, do yer," he said to George. "Yer don't know the first bloody thing about it. Last time I did the lousy job I was bitten to death by fleas and then I took 'em 'ome and the perishers bit me missus to death. I was so bloody unpopular that I'll never do the bloody job again."

After the Swan Hunter takeover and its consequent top management changes, the inevitable feeling of uncertainty had been apparent at all levels. On the appointment of H. W. Denny as works manager Tom Laing became liaison engineer between Works and Drawing Office. A new maintenance engineer was appointed, one Harry Marston, an unusual character who had trained at the Slade School of Art and was a most talented painter. One of his fellow students was W. Heath Robinson, whose fantasy engineering cartoons have become synonymous with bodgery. There is no evidence that Harry's maintenance techniques owed anything to his illustrious contemporary.

The port Cheetah IX engine of an Oxford Mk.I. *Airspeed Limited*

Said to be an Airspeed test pilot! The result of a joker's meeting with a misleading sign at the Airspeed works.

One of his burdens was a rather temperamental lavatory attendant, a dedicated craftsman whose brass, copper and porcelain gleamed brightly. George Twyman met the man looking very miserable. To George's enquiry as to the reason for his unhappiness he said that he had decided to leave the company. When George expressed the view that he was far too valuable a man to be allowed to leave for no apparent reason, the man replied, with considerable asperity, "I SHALL leave, I'm fed up with aeroplanes." The argument was unanswerable, so he left.

As in so many engineering works, there were many anonymous and surprising talents. George Twyman, seconded for a time to personnel work, soon discovered that there was musical talent in abundance. A works choir was formed. This became well patronised in Portsmouth, particularly when accompanied by the Royal Marines Orchestra from Eastney Barracks.

Even such events as this raised problems. One of the woodworkers, asked by his wife to buy two tickets, arrived home with a tale that all had been sold. His tone of voice triggered off the alarm system which ladies seem to develop, and she asked a girl friend to see what she could do. The friend had no trouble in buying tickets, so both the ladies went to the concert to find themselves seated two rows behind the gay Lothario and his lady friend. The scandalised wife left immediately in high dudgeon, no doubt in the words of Robbie Burns "To nurse her wrath and keep it warm."

An Oxford Mk.I of the first production batch ready for take-off at South Cerney, Gloucestershire.
Aeroplane Monthly

The choir was trained to very high musical standards by Fred Bennett, a sheet metal worker. On a number of occasions they sang at the King's Theatre, Southsea, accompanied by the Royal Marines Orchestra under Captain Vivian Dunn, then Director of Music of the Royal Marines. Regular musical events took place in the Flight Shed, the stage being erected on two "Queen Mary" low-loaders normally used for the transport of aeroplanes. Lunch-time concerts were held in the Works Canteen, a grand piano being borrowed from the King's Theatre.

Serious dissension arose in the Board Room in 1937 as Oxfords were beginning to flow off the production line. Norway felt that the era of adventurous projects which had characterised the company was at an end under the very conservative control of Swan Hunter. By July of that year orders in hand amounted to £594,000, and the overdraft was £104,000. Paradoxically the value of the shares began to slump, presumably because investors realised that Ministry contracts on a "cost plus" basis would certainly not produce profits sufficient to recoup past losses.

Never an easy man to work with, Norway's relationship with Hessell Tiltman began to deteriorate and Board arguments were commonplace. Tiltman was a very calm person and such friction was quite alien to his temperament. By the spring of 1938 he had decided to resign, and informed Lord Grimthorpe accordingly.

Grimthorpe, although no longer chairman, was a substantial shareholder, and he was appalled by this development. On 15th April he wrote a very sharp and critical letter expressing his great disappointment and sense of shock that "You of all people should throw your hand in when difficulties arise. I should have thought that from feelings of loyalty and good faith you at least would have stuck to the ship and done your utmost to put her into shipshape order, whoever else might leave . . . I am profoundly upset by your attitude and consider that you have badly let down your backers amongst whom I include myself, as I was the first to support you. I hope it is not yet too late for you to reconsider your attitude and for the Managers of Airspeed to resume their former happy relationship".

Loyalty and straight dealing being two of Tiltman's strongest characteristics, he was very shaken by this onslaught. His decision had been based on the assumption that Norway held all the cards, an assumption which was challenged when Tiltman decided to put to the Board that there was no longer room in the company for the two founders. The problem which then faced the Board was to decide which man could be more easily replaced. It had to conclude that there were many more competent managing directors than aircraft designers.

Norway helped them by announcing that he was interested in adopting a full-time career as a novelist. His book *Ruined City* had been published and the film rights purchased; a generous "golden handshake" by the Board made him a fairly wealthy man and he left the company he had formed in 1930 with orders in hand worth £1,262,000 and 1,035 people on the payroll. He saw an order for 200 Oxfords placed with de Havillands and departed with the thought which he quotes in *Slide Rule*: "I was learning what a better man than I had learned before me, that to travel hopefully is a better thing than to arrive, and the true success is to labour."

Hessell Tiltman was appointed managing director. Relations between him and Norway remained strained until Norway died in Australia in 1962.

In 1938 the imminence of war became abundantly clear. The Prime Minister, Neville Chamberlain, flew to Munich to meet Adolf Hitler and returned bearing the piece of paper which he stated "would give peace in our time".

Portsmouth seemed a very "jumpy" city, with sandbags appearing around many buildings and air raid shelters under construction. The defences of the whole area were being strengthened and searchlights were located in strategic places. To give much-needed experience to the searchlight crews private owners were invited to volunteer for night flying duty from the aerodrome, which was not properly lit for such activities; car headlights, suitably located, were the only landing aids whilst the AIRSPEED neon sign on the factory wall was a useful beacon.

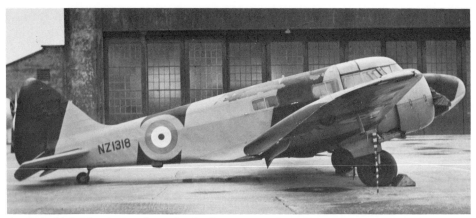

An Oxford Mk.I for the Royal New Zealand Air Force. Altogether 297 machines were delivered to New Zealand. *Aeroplane Monthly*

A Puss Moth was exercising on a dark night, the pilot often having to fly towards the beams to give the unhappy crews a little encouragement. On his return he was dismayed to find a blanket of ground mist concealing the aerodrome, although fortunately the sign blazed out. He oriented himself on this and made his let-down into the murk. Sadly, he was slightly premature and landed on the football field at the aerodrome boundary. With remarkable precision, considering the conditions, he scored a goal, hurtling through the posts and carrying them and the net across the field and on to the aerodrome, where he stepped out of the wreck almost uninjured but rather shaken.

Worse was to come, however. A man trying to find his way home along the perimeter path and using the wire fence as a guide, heard the commotion in the distance and leaned hard upon the wire in an attempt to peer through the murk. The aerodrome fire brigade had also noticed the crash and sudden silence. Taking a rough bearing on the noise, they hurtled into the darkness.

They too scored a goal, striking the fence at high speed a few yards from the unsuspecting walker. The wire tightened like a bow string and the unfortunate man found himself in the air accelerating towards Langstone Harbour; he landed on the grass, breaking an arm. The crash crew, hearing the groaning and swearing, rushed over to what they assumed to be the victim of the plane crash. They were soon better informed and hurried off to find their rightful customer.

This unfortunate contretemps kept some local lawyers happy for a considerable time.

After the R.A.F. trials of the Oxford at Upavon, deliveries were made to U.K. Flying Training Schools. By the outbreak of war in September 1939, the type was in service at No. 2 F.T.S., Brize Norton, No. 3 F.T.S., South Cerney, No. 11 F.T.S., Shawbury, and No. 14 F.T.S., Cranfield.

The sheer volume of flying over England required drastic action to reduce the number of training sorties, and the Empire Air Training Scheme was conceived to train aircrew in the empty skies of Canada, New Zealand, Australia and South Africa. In August 1938, the first of the Oxfords for the New Zealand Air Force had been shipped out to Auckland under the supervision of Walter Locke. NZ 250 was transported by lighter from the ship to Hobsonville R.N.Z.A.F. training station, where it was test flown by Wing Commander Hodson within three days of arrival. It was later flown 680 miles (1,095 km) to the Flying Training School at Wigram, Christchurch, where it immediately went into service. Later deliveries were used for instruction in navigation and aerial photography. One machine, equipped with an automatic pilot and used for survey work, flew from Hobsonville to Christchurch in 3 hours 40 minutes, a record flight for an aircraft of its type.

After the success of the first five machines, a further 111 were diverted from R.A.F. production, and as the Empire Air Training Scheme expanded rapidly the demand throughout the Commonwealth became more than Portsmouth could cope with alone. The Air Ministry built the great "shadow factory" at Christchurch, controlled by Airspeed. Another 1,515 Oxfords were produced by de Havilland at Hatfield; Standard Motors at Coventry built 750 and 1,360 were

The prototype Oxford Mk.V with Pratt and Whitney Wasp Junior engines and constant speed propellers. *Aeroplane Monthly*

built by Percival Aircraft at Luton. With Portsmouth's 4,411 and 550 from Christchurch, the total production of this remarkable trainer was 8,586.

In 1940 Oxfords were crated and sent to the Dominions. Canada received 188 airframes which were equipped with Pratt and Whitney Wasp Juniors and designated Oxford Mk V. South Africa received over 500 machines and New Zealand 297.

Some diehard aeronautical engineers looked with extreme scepticism upon wooden aircraft in the tropics. There was serious trouble with the early production models built with casein based adhesives, and under heavy humidity conditions joints grew a fungoid mould. Later, resin-based cements were used and little further trouble was experienced.

Training overseas introduced its own serious problems for pilots returning to the "clag"-ridden skies of Britain after hours of flying in clear skies. Advanced Training Units were formed to "convert" them to British weather.

In poor visibility the Standard Beam Approach system was used to bring operational aircraft in, but many hours of training were required to achieve proficiency in this difficult art. The first S.B.A. School was formed at Watchfield, equipped with Oxfords, as were the other 100 or so Beam Approach Training Flights which were attached to Advanced Flying Units and Heavy Conversion Units. All Beam Approach Training aircraft were marked with yellow triangles on the fuselage sides.

The first British aircraft used by the United States Air Force in Europe was an Oxford. The Portuguese Air Force also operated a number of them, as did the Free French, Royal Egyptian, Turkish and Iranian Air Forces.

The Canadian production run commenced in 1939, when 25 airframes were shipped out for assembly by Canadian Vickers, later renamed Canadair, at Montreal. Ron Clear, having successfully steered the Oxford through its trials at Upavon and subsequently at all other Flying Training Schools, was the obvious choice to supervise the work.

For one who was not a test pilot, although he had flown many hours with George Errington, the assignment was not an easy one. The Canadian pilots found out the characteristics of the type by trial and error. When Clear realised that an error was about to be made he had to restrict himself to a calm and diplomatic suggestion that "U.K. pilots find that the aeroplane has a tendency to swing when the throttle is opened," whilst he furtively jabbed the rudder pedals and unobtrusively adjusted the throttle to stop the incipient ground loop.

On his return from this mission Alfred Townsley decided that his diplomacy, tact and skill was worthy of recognition by training him to become a fully fledged test pilot.

In 1943 the Oxford virtually replaced the Westland Lysander in Anti-Aircraft Co-operation Squadrons as "targets" for A.A. batteries and the

A formation of Oxford Mk.Is with upper surfaces camouflaged flying from R.A.F. South Cerney in July, 1939. In the distance is a Hawker Hart trainer. *Aeroplane Monthly*

calibration of radar stations. In this boring and unglamorous role the type remained in service until the early 1950s. The Fleet Air Arm also used the machine for various duties, mainly communications.

Apart from coastal patrol work in 1940, the only known involvement of the Oxford in the shooting war was in 1941 when Rashid Ali, an Iraqi politician strongly in sympathy with Nazi Germany, overthrew the Regent and proclaimed himself Dictator of Iraq. Rebel forces began to move towards an important British base, No. 4 Flying Training School at R.A.F. Habbaniya, a grim and lonely outpost near the Euphrates river. A peacetime station, it was well equipped with modern living quarters, swimming pools and hangars but had few defences other than a strong perimeter fence, an under-strength squadron of Gladiator fighters and a detachment of Iraqi troops. The training aircraft were a mixed bag of Oxfords, Fairey Gordons, Hawker Hinds and Audaxes, the "''art with an 'ook.''

Under the pretext of carrying out manoeuvres the rebels adopted a menacing posture around the camp which, at the time, was said by Lord Tedder to be of vital importance in the Desert War. An ultimatum was issued by the Iraqis and a counter-ultimatum by the R.A.F.

Rapidly the trainer aircraft were converted for an offensive role. Battle was joined and for five days the beleaguered airmen fought day and night against very heavy odds. In a letter to the author, Air Vice Marshal A. G. Dudgeon, C.B.E., D.F.C., who was a squadron commander at Habbaniya, gave a vivid description of this remarkable battle, with the aircraft being parked behind hangars and commencing their take-off run between them to ensure a reasonable height as they passed over the gun emplacements.

At night the only lights used were the landing lights of the machines, which were snapped on as the altimeter read 50 feet (15.2m), the pilot praying that the ground thus illuminated was the aerodrome surface. Continuously under fire, they flew bombing and strafing raids with the Oxfords carrying bombs and reconnaissance cameras. On the sixth day the Iraqis gave up and retreated to Baghdad, being attacked all the way by the R.A.F.

During the operation student pilots of L.A.C. rank were employed as bomb aimers in the Oxfords. On one sortie a pilot was hit and had to be removed from his seat. The student was about to take over when the senior N.C.O. gunner came forward and ordered him out of the way, taking over and landing the machine. The N.C.O. was given a D.F.M. for his action. Air Vice Marshal Dudgeon's comment was "A very fine piece of work for a non-pilot, and he earned his D.F.M., but in the circumstances, totally unnecessary and very dangerous."

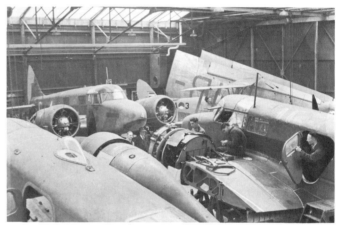

Oxfords of the Royal Netherlands Air Force being serviced at the Fokker works at Schiphol.
Aeroplane Monthly

It is fitting that the last word on the Oxford should be said by one of the Commonwealth Air Forces who ensured such high standards of flying by those R.A.F. pilots who were trained in the Empire scheme.

The South African Air Force journal *Wings* said, in January 1945, "As an operational trainer between single and twin-engined bombers the Airspeed Oxford is probably more extensively used than any other Allied trainer of this type. Practically every bomber and twin-engined fighter pilot of today has much of his early experience in this stalwart of the Commonwealth Air Training Scheme. Throughout the Empire, including the Union of South Africa, the Oxford is not only the essential link between the E.F.T.S. and the O.T.U. but also serves valiantly as a personal transport and air ambulance . . .

"The airframe is one of the most accessible in service, there are very few parts which are difficult to reach, a fault so common to the many new aeroplanes now in service. Inspections can be finished within a day by a gang of four men provided the snags are not too great. For major inspections most Air Schools organise a system of gangs to deal with each aircraft in turn. Generally this amounts to fuselage, cockpit, mainplane, tail unit and undercarriage; using this system with a total of some thirty riggers one Union Air School despatched a total of twenty-six major inspections within a single month. The simplicity of the Oxford is in every way responsible for this rapidity in spite of its wooden construction sometimes falling foul of the South African sun.

"In flying, the Oxford is one of the simplest twin-engined types. Provided the engines are synchronised and the trimming carefully adjusted hands-off flying can be done for distances up to 200 miles. For night flying the Oxford has proved highly suitable, with good visibility from the cockpit and powerful landing lights making it one of the best trainers for this work. The Oxford is a good load carrier and is capable of taking off with ten people on board from an aerodrome nearly 5,000 feet above sea level.

It's a good landing if you can crawl away from it! An Oxford Mk.II at 34 F.T.S., Abingdon, Canada, on 13th April, 1941.
Aeroplane Monthly

"Most aeroplanes experience conflicting criticism, both good and bad, the Oxford is no exception. Many will say it is a bad machine for steep turns and a tendency to spin, others including test pilots, swear by its manoeuvrability and one Squadron Leader stated that he would rather do aerobatics in an Oxford than in a Tiger Moth. He carried out some very unofficial demonstrations, some at night. Loops, rolls and inverted flying of brief duration seemed to create no unusual disturbance except in the minds of those who did not think it could be done.

"A fine example of Oxford stability even after a mid-air collision appeared in the English press recently. Two photographs showed the remains of a tailplane which amounted to about 75% of the normal area, despite this damage, and with no elevators and a badly damaged fin, the Oxford was successfully flown back to its base. Another unfortunate Oxford which got in the way of granite blasting, flew back to the station on three longerons.

"In Canada, operating under icy conditions, Oxfords were found to suffer severely from cracked cylinders, subsequently the engine was shielded com-

The prototype Oxford Mk.V photographed in May, 1942. The camouflage scheme is the same as in the picture on page 109 but the markings have undergone considerable change.

Airspeed Limited

pletely by a circular disc to prevent ice hitting the hot cylinders. There was no ill-effect upon the cooling of the motor. Oxfords have also been flown in extreme heat without any engine cowlings, although this led to a considerable loss of speed.

"Mishaps often had fatal results, particularly in night flying training. The Oxford burned very easily and very quickly, although the fitting of rubber-clad tanks assisted in reducing fuel spillage and the number of casualties through fire. One pilot is said to have saved his life in an Oxford when almost uncontrollable at ground level by managing to steer it between two adjacent buildings on the aerodrome so that both wings were torn off on the buildings, to burn themselves out harmlessly whilst he careered on in the fuselage.''

Probably the most tragic accident to befall an Oxford occurred in January 1941, when Amy Johnson was lost in the Thames Estuary. Eleven years earlier she had electrified the world by flying alone to Australia in a single-engined de Havilland Moth with no radio. She was one of the world's outstanding woman navigators, and, as a ferry pilot in Air Transport Auxiliary, was flying an Oxford from Blackpool to an aerodrome near Oxford. The weather was extremely bad with fog and low cloud.

She appeared to have lost her bearings and run out of fuel over the Estuary. A trawler, H.M.S. *Haslemere*, spotted a parachutist descending into the sea and then an aircraft circling silently before crashing into the water. The trawler made for the spot where the parachutist was seen to drop, but ran aground momentarily, just long enough to make it impossible to rescue what the crew recognised as a woman. The trawler's skipper, Lieutenant Commander Walter

Fletcher, dived into the freezing sea in an heroic attempt to rescue Amy; he died of exposure. So they both perished, amid a welter of speculation that there was a mystery passenger. In recent years speculation has been revived with the suggestion that she was, in fact, on a secret mission into occupied France.

Throughout the war the Oxford performed magnificently in most theatres of operation. After the war hundreds became surplus to requirements as the Royal Air Force contracted. Many were posted to Fighter Command when the Gloster Meteor and de Havilland Hornet day fighters, both twin-engined, were to be flown by pilots who hitherto had flown single-engined machines. Very high standards of instrument flying were required for these very fast fighters, so 11 Group and 12 Group set up their own squadrons, No. 1 at Tangmere and No. 41 at Church Fenton, equipped them with Harvards and Oxfords, and charged them with the task of achieving the highest possible standards of instrument flying for the Groups.

When the Auxiliary Air Force was re-formed and equipped with Mosquitoes, Oxfords were used for instrument training and conversion. In 1952 the Korean War caused a resurgence of training and new Advanced Schools were equipped with Oxfords.

Oxford LX 119 was fitted with Alvis Leonides engines by Miles Aircraft at Woodley in 1947. Nine years earlier Airspeed had fitted a Leonides engine to a Bristol Bulldog in which the engine was type tested. No further versions of this Oxford were built.

The production life of the type had ended on 14th July 1945, when the 4,411th and last Oxford to be built at Portsmouth was demonstrated there in company with the eighth of the first production batch, L 4542. This machine had been delivered in January 1938, and had been flown throughout the war, a remarkable record for a wooden aeroplane in such a taxing job as training and an achievement that reflects immense credit upon Hessell Tiltman and his design and production teams.

After the Korean emergency had passed the Oxfords, like old soldiers, just faded away. For some of them a new lease of life was ahead as either a civil conversion in a rudimentary sense or as the full A.S.65 Consul small air liner.

Oxford LX.119 fitted with Alvis Leonides engines in 1947. *Alvis Limited*

At a meeting of the Airspeed Policy Committee as far back as 16th April 1940, Sir Alan Cobham had given his views on the company's policy to be adopted on the cessation of hostilities. Bill Shaylor thought that Airspeed could form a powerful sales organisation to compete in world markets and that the conversion of Oxfords to civil use would be a valuable stopgap until a new design could be put into production. Airspeeds should negotiate with the Government to buy back new and low-hour machines, and those under construction, with the object of taking advantage of the low price which he expected to pay for war surplus equipment. His market survey also envisaged the emergence of the executive transport, a new concept at the time.

Shaylor's predictions were remarkably accurate. Airspeed were able to buy the machines very cheaply, modifications to meet Civil Certification requirements were minimal and a very attractive, if rather noisy, four/five seat fully-equipped airliner, the Consul, was offered for the very reasonable price of £5,500, with a good profit for Airspeed.

A longer nose, hinged to give access to the baggage compartment, and an extra window in the fuselage sides were the main visual changes. A readjustment of the tail plane incidence enabled the centre of gravity limit to be moved further forward, giving more flexibility in loading and improving fore-and-aft stability.

An ambulance version was produced with an upward opening door giving access for two stretchers and one or two sitting patients. Other variants were an executive transport with four seats and a lavatory, and a convertible machine with a large door for loading freight.

Rocket launchers and machine guns fitted to the Oxfords ordered by the Burmese Government in 1949. *Airspeed Limited*

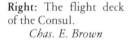

Above: The A.S.65 Consul, an airliner conversion of the Oxford.
Flight

Right: The flight deck of the Consul.
Chas. E. Brown

A military version was ordered by the Burmese Government in 1949. Three R.A.F. Oxfords were converted to mount two forward firing .303 calibre machine guns and eight 25 lb (11.3 kg) rocket projectiles, and one of the original Armstrong Whitworth dorsal turrets with a Lewis gun was fitted. These were test flown by Bob Milne and checked at R.A.E. Farnborough before being flown out to Burma. The turret, which had not been seen for a number of years on Oxfords, vividly reminded Bob of one of his most embarrassing moments when he took off in a Mark I complete with turret and landed as a Mark II, minus turret but plus a draught, the turret having become detached in flight and sucked out of the fuselage.

Virtually the only profitable aeroplanes built by Airspeed were the Oxford and Consul. By the time the Consul was in production the company was a wholly owned subsidiary of de Havilland and was able to take advantage of the world marketing activities of its powerful parent.

CHAPTER FIVE

Queen Wasp and Other Projects

EXPERIMENTS with wireless controlled aeroplanes, to use the quaint terminology of the period, began during the First World War with varying degrees of success, although little information was released until the summer of 1935.

One of the first successful machines was a specially converted Fairey IIIF with increased dihedral to give inherent lateral stability. It also had a large squared-off fin and rudder and looked so extraordinary that crowds gathered at Lee on Solent whenever it flew. It was ultimately shot down by the guns of H.M.S. *Sussex* in a Mediterranean shoot.

In 1934 a converted de Havilland Tiger Moth, called Queen Bee, became the standard target aircraft in use with the Navy Gunnery Co-operation Flights. Considerable controversy raged in high places as to the ability of bombers to hit warships from high altitude. Undoubtedly there were some diehard naval officers who judged the bomber's potential in terms of the performance of this insignificant little aeroplane, and of other Fleet Air Arm types, and were lulled into a sense of false security which probably led to the catastrophic naval losses through dive bombing in the early years of the Second World War.

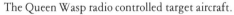

The Queen Wasp radio controlled target aircraft.

At sea the Queen Bee was launched by catapult. The Control Officer had before him a small control panel with press-buttons for each function. With the engine running he would carry out his "cockpit checks" by pressing each button in turn and observing the control response. The Catapult Release Officer would then fire the catapult and the aircraft would climb slowly to the height required by the Gunnery Officer. The shoot would then begin.

Visual range was the only limitation, and the Control Officer would be equipped with an enormous pair of binoculars. In exceptional visibility the Bee could be flown up to 15 miles (24 km) from the ship.

The Royal Air Force operated Nos. 1, 2 and 3 Anti-aircraft Co-operation Units at Biggin Hill, Lee-on-Solent and Malta. It soon became clear that the results obtained in Queen Bee shoots, poor though they were, were quite unrepresentative of active service conditions. The maximum speed of the machine was only 109 m.p.h. (175 km/hr).

Airspeed were invited in 1935 to tender for a Queen Bee replacement to Specification Q32/35. The specification called for a high-performance machine small enough for stowage aboard and launching from a warship. Folding wings were therefore necessary, and simple conversion from wheel to float undercarriage was essential whilst the aeroplane should be inherently stable and easily controlled.

The Air Ministry required the tender to be submitted as quickly as possible, so Hessell Tiltman set up a special drawing office in London Road,

Bringing a Queen Bee target aircraft on board after a flight, a rather undignified process.
via Aeroplane Monthly

The second prototype Queen Wasp on floats. *Aeroplane Monthly*

Portsmouth, so that work could proceed without the day-to-day distractions of the main factory. As a result, the prototype flew nine months after design work commenced.

The design team decided that one of the most important factors was ease of handling on catapults at sea and ashore, which meant that size and weight must be reduced to the minimum. Moreover, salvage was a problem with such a machine, so small size was an all-round advantage. A biplane layout was indicated; an analysis of the speed penalty of this configuration revealed a difference of around 5 m.p.h. (8 km/hr) by comparison with a monoplane layout. The operational altitude for the type was 10,000 feet (3,000m). The smallest and cheapest engine to give the required performance was the Wolseley Scorpio Mk II. This choice of engine offered another advantage, as its supply to Airspeed would not interfere with the heavy demands on the aero engine industry created by the expansion programme of the Royal Air Force and the Fleet Air Arm. Lord Nuffield's decision to terminate aero engine production was a severe blow to Airspeed, who were forced to redesign the project around the Armstrong Siddeley Cheetah IX 350 h.p. radial engine.

The structure was primarily of wood, the forward section of the fuselage being a very strong spruce and ply assembly which provided the centre sections for upper and lower mainplanes and carried the welded steel tubular engine mounting. On the lower centre section were the strongpoints for the undercarriage mounting and the forward catapult spools. The rear fuselage was a semi-monocoque structure of spruce longerons and stiffeners, ply covered, with a fabric-on-stringers fairing on the top surface merging into the ply covered fin built integrally with the rear fuselage.

The mainplanes were sharply tapered, a surprising feature in a machine designed for remote control. They were of twin-spar ply-covered construction, interconnected by a single strut on each side, the bracing wires being in the plane of the front spar. The tailplane was of similar construction, with rudder and elevators of spruce, fabric covered.

The controls were complex. Airspeed had already carried out considerable research into slow-flying control problems with the R.A.F. Courier K 4047, which they converted in 1934 to have slotted flaps outboard of the centre section and Schrenk flaps inboard, with the additional ability to lower the ailerons symmetrically to augment the flap area. Further work had also been done on the A.S.27 slow-speed coastal patrol project, which was not built. The lessons learned from these two designs were embodied in the target machine.

Access to the cockpit was through a door on the starboard side between the main bulkheads. A transparent sliding panel in the cockpit roof gave access to the slinging gear and wing locking pins, as well as serving as an emergency exit.

The whole concept of pilotless flight was remarkably advanced at this time, with an array of fail-safe devices to cope with every predictable malfunction. The basic control medium was an air-powered gyro system directing pneumatic servos to the rudder and elevators. No aileron control was used in automatic flight. Coded Morse signals from the transmitter were fed into the gyro by pneumatic pistons and limited throttle control was available in three positions, full open, cruise power and closed. A complex throttle control override protected it from the effect of acceleration forces on the gyro causing misleading signals to be received.

To land the machine "landing glide" was selected on the control panel. As soon as the speed dropped to the correct figure a servo motor lowered the flaps, and the landing sequence began when a weight on the end of the trailing aerial touched the ground, closing contacts on the aerial winch which selected "elevator up" and switched off the gyro.

In bumpy weather aerial snatch could activate the landing sequence inadvertently, so it was necessary to include a further interlock to ensure that the signal could not become operative before the "landing glide" signal had been received.

If a major control failure occurred the aircraft would be set into a gliding turn to port so that a reasonable landing might be made, hopefully, in a safe area. In the event of radio failure the glide turn procedure was initiated if an interval of two minutes elapsed without radio signals.

One of the problems of radio control was revealed at a lunch in the de Havilland Board Room at Hatfield when Hessell Tiltman was discussing the Queen Bee during the design stage of the Airspeed machine. He said that he had heard of a strange incident when a Queen Bee pilot had been briefed to carry out tests at Martlesham to monitor the input signals. The Control Officer agreed that he would cease transmission at midday and the pilot would return for lunch in the Mess. At 12 o'clock the pilot was surprised to find the aeroplane becoming distinctly skittish and performing some rather advanced aerobatics which were slowly destroying his interest in lunch. After twenty minutes of this he decided that, rather than ask an erk to clean out the cockpit, he should switch off and go home.

Ashen faced, he found the Control Officer and rather indignantly demanded an explanation of the aerobatic display. The man was mystified. He declared that he had switched off at the agreed hour and that no transmission was going out.

Further tests were laid on at the same time the following day and it was found that, as the transmission ceased, the receiver picked up a dance band programme from Radio Paris.

None of the de Havilland executives at lunch had ever heard this story, but confirmation was not slow in coming. "I can vouch for it," said an R.A.F. group captain in the party. "I was the pilot!"

The new machine was to have been called the "Clay Pigeon". Fortunately wiser counsels prevailed and it became the Queen Wasp. The only minor problem which arose at the assembly stage was the location of the hand starter gear on the wrong side so that the unfortunate erk or matelot starting the machine by turning the large handle ran a grave risk of a sharp clout on the rump by a propeller blade as the engine fired. It was relatively simple to move the unit to the other side.

Two prototypes, K.8887 on wheels and K.8888 on floats, were completed. The first flew in the record time of 13 weeks from issue of drawings. George Errington flew the silver doped K.8887 for the first time on 11th June 1937, and the flight was entirely satisfactory. The second machine on floats was to have been tested by a well-known test pilot experienced in marine aircraft, but at the last minute he withdrew. Cyril Colman, with no experience of float planes, carried out a completely successful first flight. Slight problems of porpoising arose but modifications to the float design soon cured them.

George Errington and Flight Lieutenant Colman continued the test programme, K.8887 on wheels being flown from Portsmouth whilst K.8888, on floats, was based at Lee-on-Solent. Handling was quite satisfactory. K.8887 appeared at the R.A.F. Display at Hendon at the end of June and the seaplane carried out catapult trials from H.M.S. *Pegasus* in November.

The introduction of the Queen Wasp to the Royal Navy was not without drama. Prior to live catapult trials the Navy decided that the aircraft should be

The Queen Wasp prototype in the New Types Park at the Hendon Air Display of June, 1937.

Aeroplane Monthly

lifted aboard *Pegasus* to check recovery procedures and ease of hoisting aboard the catapult. To check the seaworthiness of the machine it was to be taxied to its rendezvous with the ship in the Channel. It was arranged that R. W. Cantello, the Wasp project engineer, should accompany Cyril Colman, who was driving the Wasp. At the last minute a *Flight* photographer joined the party to record the event, so he and Cantello went in a speedboat.

After a miserable trip in choppy seas they were dismayed to find that the Navy was distinctly hostile, as they were said to have arrived a day too early. It was out of the question to lower a companion ladder to permit them to embark, but after wet and fruitless attempts at boarding in full view of contemptuously laughing naval ratings, they finally crawled up rope ladders, sodden and frightened out of their wits. Relations between the landlubbers and the Navy improved in the wardroom, and the tests were satisfactorily completed.

Later in November the seaplane K.8888 was successfully launched from H.M.S. *Pegasus* and Service trials began in earnest.

An unfortunate contretemps occurred at Farnborough during catapult trials. K.8888, its floats exchanged for wheels, was mounted ready for its first launch with Flight Lieutenant McDougall in charge. The catapult was fired and the Wasp rose gracefully into the air, but there was no sign of the pilot.

The second prototype Queen Wasp at Farnborough after a catapult launch that went wrong.
Aeroplane Monthly

The machine dived slightly, bounced a wheel and rose again to drop the other wheel on the ground. After this bounce the wing tip hit and dug in, the aircraft rolling right over and wrecking itself.

Onlookers, fearful of fire, rushed over, to find the pilot shouting for release from the rear fuselage. He was quickly removed, soaked in fuel but otherwise almost uninjured. He had been despatched to the rear when the acceleration forces of the catapult launch had proved too much for the seat anchorage, made with mild steel bolts instead of the high tensile steel bolts specified. McDougall was an extremely lucky man.

Two developments of the Queen Wasp were envisaged, the A.S.38 communications aircraft and the A.S.50 trainer to Specification T24/40. No work was carried out on either.

A small factory at Langstone Harbour was opened under the control of Tom Laing, and production of the first batch of Wasps began there. Only four or five were built before the contract was cancelled, however.

Hessell Tiltman recalled a strange incident during the flight test programme. George Errington had carried out stalling tests on K.8887 and walked into Tiltman's office saying, "I would like you to come up in this aeroplane with me to see a very odd characteristic." In Tiltman's own words, "I climbed into the compartment where the radio was usually fitted. George said 'Will you please check the following facts; you will see that we are at 2,000 feet, vertically over the edge of the aerodrome on the leeward side. Please watch carefully; I shall pull the stick back until the wings have an angle of attack right on the other side of the stall.' ''

Tiltman saw the air speed indicator reading drop to 45 m.p.h. (72 km/hr) and, gradually, to zero.

''In the meantime we were losing height very rapidly indeed. Noticing the expression of anxiety on my face Errington assured me that the machine was under proper control, which he demonstrated by putting on full aileron. The machine responded by rocking gently as it would do under normal flying conditions. To get into the aerodrome the pilot had to put the nose well down and open the engine to full throttle. We just skimmed the hedge.

''While in the super-stalled condition we must have descended vertically, indeed I think we were going astern in the ten-knot wind. During the descent the attitude was normal, say plus five to ten degrees, but the angle of attack must have been nearer eighty degrees. This confounded the theory that sharply tapered wings are unstable in the stall and tend to drop sharply. The machine was particularly stable laterally at all speeds with flaps up and rudder central.''

It was possible to reproduce this phenomenon on K.8887 very easily, but not on K.8888 or the later production models. Indeed the few production models built attracted some criticism from pilots who found that the stalling

''The Powers That Be'' from the *Airspeed Gazette*, Christmas 1939. H. W. Denny has the Queen Wasp on the pond, Alfred Townsley tows the landplane version, and J. Liddell and Hessell Tiltman discuss the Oxford and the missing bonus.

~ The Powers That Be ~

characteristics were rather vicious. It would appear that the condition was an extremely critical one which minor modifications or production tolerances in the centre section altered completely.

It is sadly ironic that George Errington, who was almost obsessed with research into stalling characteristics and, in the above episode, probably encountered the first super-stall, should have met his death in 1966 as co-pilot of a de Havilland Trident on a test flight when the stall was being explored. Recovery was delayed too long, the machine entered a super-stall in which the high tail was blanketed by the wing wash. The Trident crashed near Norwich killing all on board.

The contract for 90 Queen Wasps was cancelled when the Luftwaffe provided targets in abundance, and the machines in construction were broken up at Hayling Island.

The second prototype Queen Wasp on floats, July, 1937.
Aeroplane Monthly

Hessell Tiltman had a very soft spot for the Wasp; of all the aircraft he designed it was his favourite. A. E. Ellison, Chief Designer at the time, thought it was ridiculously complicated and expensive for the job it had to do. Nevertheless, within the limits of the specification to which it was designed it was a very efficient and handsome aeroplane which, like every other Airspeed aeroplane with the exception of the Horsa and Oxford, was not allowed to develop its full potential.

Alvis Limited, the Coventry car manufacturers, had decided to enter the aero engine business and had negotiated a contract to produce under licence a range of radial engines made in France. The first of these, the Alvis Leonides, was a 450 h.p. radial engine. It was to be type tested to obtain Air Ministry approval. Airspeed were invited to carry out the work in a two-seater version of the famous Bristol Bulldog fighter, normally fitted with the 490 h.p. Bristol Jupiter VII F radial engine. The power/weight ratio of the Alvis engine was so good that the engine bearers had to be extended about two feet to ensure that the centre of gravity was in the correct position.

George Errington flew the Bulldog on every possible occasion. Great care had to be observed on take-off as the propeller clearance with tail up was only three inches, but the only trouble ever experienced was the loss of the propeller spinner over Langstone Harbour. George was puzzled why it should fall off in this way, and flew low over the sandbanks at low tide. He spotted what he thought was the spinner on a bank in the middle of the harbour and rushed back to the aerodrome, boarded his own B. A. Swallow, a Pobjoy-engined low-wing monoplane, ideal for such an escapade, and landed on the sandbank to find to his dismay that the ''spinner'' was an oil drum. The very observant safety authorities at the harbour saw the Swallow plunging into the water and immediately mobilised a rescue crew which, in turn, was astounded to see it apparently rise out of the sea and fly away.

In a very rash moment Errington flew the Bulldog through a massive cumulo-nimbus cloud at 17,000 feet to demonstrate to John Marlow, the Alvis

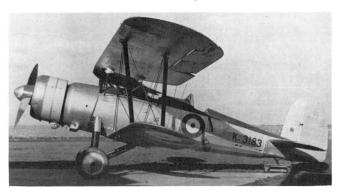

The Bristol Bulldog in which Airspeed installed an Alvis Leonides engine for flight testing.
Alvis Limited

engineer, something which George himself had not experienced, the immense natural power unleashed in such clouds, power which has frequently ripped aeroplanes apart. He thought that as the Bulldog had been built to fighter standards of strength there would be no problem.

There were problems, however. Icing was the first one, the struts, pivot head for the air speed indicator and the venturi driving the blind flying instruments being immediate casualties. George was certain that he could fly this old timer by the seat of his pants and just relaxed, until an alarmed shout from the observer and a tightening of his harness indicated that all was not well. He looked round to see Marlow surrounded by leads apparently rising vertically out of the cockpit. He suddenly realised that they were inverted and diving fast for the ground. They shot out of the cloud to find Chichester Cathedral almost overhead and horribly close. They rolled out and flew home. George concluded that if one flies old crates by the seat of one's pants, one should always make quite certain that seat of pants is in contact with old crate all the time.

After the war the Leonides was used in several aircraft, and found its level as a helicopter power plant. It is not known what happened to the Bulldog.

One of the odder aeronautical sights and sounds on the south coast in 1940 was the Airspeed A.S.39 Fleet Shadower. Heralded by the waspish sound of its four small radial engines, it could be seen scuttling around Portsmouth demonstrating its ability to fly much more slowly than any of its contemporaries, and indeed, when the wind was blowing at more than 35 m.p.h. (56 km/hr), actually proceeding, in nautical parlance, "slow astern".

A minimum flying speed of 35 m.p.h. was achieved by the expedient of "hanging on the slipstream" created by the four propellers distributed along the leading edge of the wing. The Shadower embodied the Crouch-Bolas principle*, developed in the U.S.A., in a multi-engined configuration with the slipstream spread along the maximum span of the wing.

In the period between the wars, when radar was barely a theory, the location of warships at sea was a chancy business. Reconnaissance aircraft such as Hawker Ospreys, Blackburn Sharks and the redoubtable Supermarine Walrus or "Shagbat" were carried in the larger warships and catapulted off. Recovery involved the ship in speed reduction to a few knots, a most hazardous undertaking in wartime and one not to be seriously considered by the Navy, who mostly looked upon aviation with barely concealed contempt. No operational land-based aircraft had the range to be effective and all were too fast to maintain contact, as indeed were the current shipborne types.

So in 1937 Specification S23/37 was issued by the Air Ministry based upon Admiralty requirements for shadowing and maintaining contact with enemy ships at sea.

W. F. "Bill" Shaylor, later to become a director of Airspeed, was involved in the early stages of the Shadower, although he was not then employed by Airspeed. He was an engineer with the Pobjoy engine company, who had provided the engines for two monoplanes, the Scion twin and the Scion Senior with four Pobjoy Niagara engines, built by Short Bros. The Admiralty were seriously considering the use of a multi-engined aircraft for fleet spotting and Shaylor accompanied Commander Caspar John, ultimately to be the first Fleet Air Arm officer to become First Sea Lord, and another officer on a flight in the Short Scion.

Shaylor had met N. S. Norway in Montreal during the visit of R.100. He had been flying reporters to and from the airship and, as Norway was carrying out market research on the original biplane project which was to launch Airspeed, they spent many hours discussing the project. They next met in 1936 at the opening of Bromma Airport in Sweden, when Norway and Cyril Colman demonstrated an Envoy.

In 1937 Airspeed's marketing activities, or the lack of them, was a matter of great concern to Norway who remembered Bill Shaylor and wrote inviting him to join the company. Shaylor was very dubious about changing from Pobjoy, who were well entrenched with Short Bros, to join a company which appeared to

*See glossary.

have little support from anyone. However, he decided to take the chance and joined them as commercial manager.

The company had received Specification S23/37 and, as the industry had learned to its dismay, the requirements of the Royal Navy were incredibly difficult to meet. A cruising speed of 38 knots was called for. A duration of six hours at cruising speed, a quite exceptional field of vision for the crew, combined with a very low noise level and the ability to be quickly struck down the lift of an aircraft carrier, presented a somewhat awesome task for the designer.

General Aircraft Limited and Airspeed were invited to submit proposals, and orders were placed for prototypes of both designs, which were remarkably similar in layout and performance. Both the General Aircraft team and Hessell Tiltman, who had recently visited the U.S.A., were familiar with work being

W. F. "Bill" Shaylor with George Errington.
Airspeed Limited

done across the Atlantic on the subject of slow flying, with particular emphasis on the Crouch Bolas experiments.

The Airspeed Courier and Envoy small airliners had been subjected to tests at Farnborough and Martlesham with various types of flap, and the data had been published in research reports on slow-speed flying.

Present-day consideration of such a specification would inevitably involve the helicopter, but in 1937 this type of aircraft was in an extremely rudimentary form, and the Autogiro was hardly taken seriously, although the Army evaluated the Avro-built Cierva C.30A in the army co-operation role. One of these machines landed on the deck of H.M.S. *Furious* on 9th September 1935, during trials with the Navy, but the type was too small and the design of large rotorcraft was not considered feasible at this time.

The span of the Shadower was restricted to 53 feet 4 inches (16.25m). Aspect ratio and wing area were conflicting requirements, so it was essential to include high lift devices which could be relied upon to operate continuously under rigorous marine operating conditions. An outstanding field of vision and adequate propeller clearance dictated a high wing layout.

Four 130 h.p. Pobjoy Niagara V seven-cylinder radial engines, each driving a fixed pitch wooden propeller 8 feet (2.4m) in diameter were installed. An 85-gallon fuel tank in the root of each wing fed two engines through dual engine-driven pumps.

Satisfactory lateral control was achieved by locating a large proportion of aileron area in the slipstream of the outer propellers. Inboard of the slotted ailerons, large slotted flaps were interconnected to them. When the flaps were lowered to 40 degrees the ailerons drooped to 15 degrees. Actuation of the flaps was pneumatic, using the same power source as the wheel brakes.

Originally the Shadower was designed with twin rudders, but wind tunnel tests at Farnborough indicated problems and a centre fin was added. Unfortunately the tests did not reveal the ineffectiveness of the elevators, which was only discovered in the air.

The fuselage was a wooden stressed skin monocoque structure built in one unit, with the observer's section as a detachable shell. The wings were of wooden construction with two spruce and plywood box spars, wooden ribs and a ply skin. The inter-spar section was watertight to provide buoyancy in the event of a ditching. Wing struts were of tubular steel, with a fixed jury strut to support the front spar when folded.

The wings folded manually about hinges located at the root. Very little effort was required to move them, although folding at sea might have presented serious problems. The tail unit was of wooden construction, the tailplane incidence being adjustable in flight.

The undercarriage was designed to obviate the possibility of a nose-over in a carrier landing. The main structure, a long oleo pneumatic shock absorber leg, radius rod and axle, were mounted well forward in a position which almost guaranteed directional instability. To correct this inherent fault a powerful self-centering device was incorporated in the shock absorber of the tail wheel.

The selection of the Pobjoy engines was a major factor in achieving a low noise level. Four small engines with geared propellers running at low tip speeds are much easier to silence than a single engine of comparable power.

The Shadower had a crew of three. The pilot's seat was on a raised deck offset to port to leave a passageway to the observer's station in the nose and to the radio operator's just forward of the rear spar bulkhead.

This bulkhead, on the mockup, caused anguish to the author, when in 1938, as a very green apprentice in the Experimental Department, he was instructed in fitting to the bulkhead the tubular steel structure which carried the wing mock up. He was enjoined by the chargehand ''Make sure the nuts are really tight, lad!'' The lad was fairly confident of their tightness when the ''penny'' washers under the nuts were slightly conical and recessed an eighth of an inch into the wood. Ralph Gover was a tolerant mentor and a consummate craftsman, but his comments are a vivid memory over 40 years later!

At a Design Meeting in February 1940, it was reported that General Aircraft were about to fly their prototype and thought that they would lose about £5,000 on each of the two machines. Airspeed's loss was expected to be about the same.

George Errington test flew the prototype, N.1323, on 18th October 1940. The results were disappointing. As was expected, the climb was very poor and elevator control left much to be desired. When the throttles were closed a large nosedown change of trim occurred, due to areas of airflow instability behind the engines being accentuated by sudden loss of slipstream airflow. In effect the wing behind the engines was in a stalled condition. The poor climb performance was due to the high drag and low power/weight ratio.

Naval and air experience of the war in the first few months and the potential inherent in experiments in radio-location, as radar was called in those days, indicated clearly that the concept embodied in the Fleet Shadower was faulty. The project was abandoned, N.1323 and the unfinished N.1324 being scrapped. This was yet another example of a military aircraft being ruined by impossible requirements.

Undoubtedly data obtained from this aircraft, particularly its ''flappery'', was used in the design of the Horsa military glider. It went part of the way to meet the famous dictum of the immortal C. G. Grey, the founder of *The Aeroplane*, who demanded aeroplanes that could fly very slowly and did not

The A.S.39 Fleet Shadower with its four Pobjoy Niagara V radial engines.   *Airspeed Limited*

burn up. Many years later, Hessell Tiltman commented to the author that the Air Ministry always came to Airspeed if they wanted a queer aeroplane. It can be said with some certainty that the Fleet Shadower was distinctly queer.

At the Design Meeting held on 8th March 1939, it was reported that Airspeed would almost certainly receive an order for two prototypes of a single-engined trainer submitted to meet Specification T.34/39. It was intended to be in the category of the Miles Master and the North American Harvard, of which there seemed a possibility of shortage as the major expansion of the training programme progressed.

The aircraft was the A.S.45 Cambridge, not one of Hessell Tiltman's more inspired designs. Officially it was dropped after the two prototypes had been completed because deliveries of Masters and Harvards were adequate. It was not, however a technical success, the structure weight being excessive due to the two car-type doors on each side. In addition, the wing section was not a good choice, giving unacceptably high drag characteristics, so the Bristol Mercury VII engine of 730 h.p. was inadequate.

The first machine, T.2249, was flown by George Errington on 19th February 1941. Most of the development flying was done by George, who had a rather alarming experience in it. Due to excessive drag, difficulty was experienced in achieving the maximum specified diving speed. On one flight he

The A.S.45 Cambridge single-engine trainer under construction. *Airspeed Limited*

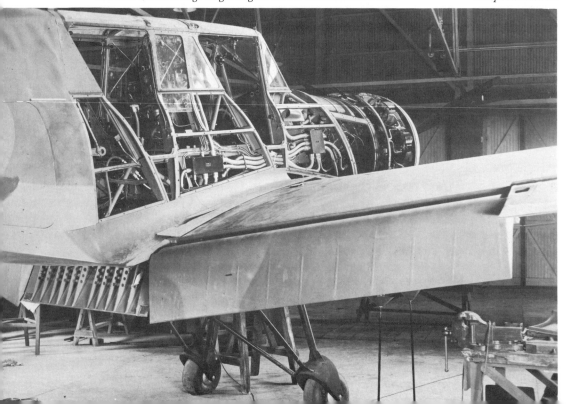

entered an almost vertical dive, and as speed built up towards 270 m.p.h. (435 km/hr), the required speed, he began to pull out. Suddenly, with a tremendous bang, the upper surface of the starboard wing about three metres out from the root disappeared. He carefully reduced power, expecting the wing to fold. To his amazement there was no change in trim down to 100 m.p.h. (160 km/hr) and he managed to land it at a rather higher speed than usual.

After another test flight Bob Milne selected undercarriage down and the starboard green light flickered. He landed it very carefully and taxied back to the flight line, turning in a series of circles to ensure that the suspect leg was always loaded outwards. He filled in the snag sheet and mentioned the trouble to Ron Clear just as George Errington, who was to take the machine up again, entered the office.

Milne told him of the trouble and warned him not to fly until the leg had been checked. "Oh!" said George. "That's all right, it has flickered with me before."

He climbed into the machine, started the engine and taxied towards the downwind end of the field as the two pilots watched apprehensively. As the Cambridge turned to starboard their worst fears were realised and the leg collapsed.

A very disconsolate Errington awaited the arrival of the crash crew, no doubt regretting his folly. It was a surprising lapse on the part of a pilot who normally was meticulous.

Milne was probably saved from a disastrous crash in this aircraft by a piece of gentle horseplay. He was about to leave on a test flight and was checking the controls. One of the other pilots walked under the wing tip to inspect the aileron hinge. Bob playfully pushed the stick across to hit him on the head with the aileron. As it hit him the control column came away from its mounting. The fixing bolts had loosened. If this had happened in the air the results would have been catastrophic.

When the decision was made to abandon the Cambridge the company was instructed to deliver the prototype to Farnborough. The paperwork was prepared and Ron Clear made the delivery flight, arriving back looking most unhappy. He had gone to the pilots' office saying "I have brought this A.S.45, the contract is finished, over to you now for handling". Nobody seemed very interested, and those present were even reluctant to sign for it. To his request for a parking site came the answer that he should continue down the perimeter track past the hangars to a point where a marshaller would guide him. On arrival at this point he was shocked to see the area covered with burnt out aeroplanes. The marshaller explained that tests on fire-fighting equipment were carried out here and, initially, the Cambridge would be used to fan the flames. Ron wondered whether the many hours of flight testing to achieve satisfactory control responses and drag reduction had been worth while.

The A.S.45 Cambridge, of which only two prototypes were built. *Airspeed Limited*

The ultimate fate of these two rather unsatisfactory aeroplanes is not known.

A pioneering venture by Airspeed was responsible for saving the lives of countless aircrew during the war.

At the Brussels Air Show in 1938 W. F. Shaylor and Cyril Colman met the British Air Attaché, who told them of a man called Bellezanne who was developing fireproof fuel tanks in Paris and who might wish to place the British licence. Realising that war was a strong possibility and that the Germans already had such tanks, the two men persuaded the Board to investigate Bellezanne's company, C.I.M.A.

Norway and Tiltman visited Paris and were very impressed by the process, the only tools required being scissors, knives, pincers, wooden hammers and needles. They also realised the difficulty of trying to persuade the Ministry that such cladding on tanks was vital to reduce aircrew casualties.

On 22nd April 1939, George Wigham Richardson, the chairman, visited C.I.M.A. and reported very favourably to the Board. It was decided to form a subsidiary company, to be known as Fireproof Tanks Limited, and to appoint Walter Locke, who had flown with Cyril Colman on the epic Envoy delivery flight to China in 1937, to manage the company.

Tiltman visited the Air Ministry to inform them of the formation of Fireproof Tanks Limited and to obtain their interest in the new development. He was received by an old adversary who had treated him in cavalier fashion over the submission of an earlier project. To his utter astonishment he was told in most condescending tones ''Mr Tiltman, we know all about it, you mind your business of building aeroplanes and we will mind ours''.

Tiltman retorted ''The Germans and the Italians use these tanks, so we must do so''.

''Just go away, Tiltman, and mind your business!'' was the discouraging answer. All work was stopped on fireproof tanks.

In December 1939, a curt letter was received from the Ministry instructing Airspeed to send a director to Harrogate for a very important conference to be held next day at which fuel tanks were to be discussed. Tiltman travelled north with Walter Locke. Once again his ''friend'' was present, but by this time he had become very interested in fireproof tanks. After a preliminary skirmish he asked how long it would take to cover some experimental tanks.

Tiltman replied ''The company had only just been formed and we dropped all work on the tanks after your sharp rebuff. We have to buy materials from Paris. If you can arrange swift transport from Paris and supply us with the tanks immediately we can finish them in about ten days''.

The civil servant was aghast: ''I did not expect to have to remind you, Tiltman, that there is a war on''. Locke and Tiltman were speechless and immediately withdrew. Three weeks later the tanks were delivered to Portsmouth for finishing.

By 1941 factories were operating in Portsmouth, Bristol, Manchester and London, with Walter Locke as managing director. During the war the company processed 250,334 tanks, with nearly 11 million square feet of cladding. F.P.T. Industries Limited still operate at Portsmouth, mainly making bag-type tanks which they developed after the war.

Airspeed was the first British aircraft factory to be bombed in the Second World War. In July 1940, a large formation of German bombers approached the south coast to bomb the Supermarine works at Southampton. Six Hurricanes were scrambled to intercept and they split the Luftwaffe formation, several aircraft jettisoning their bombs in their haste to escape the avenging fighters. Two bombs fell in the middle of the tool room machine shop area, fortunately after working hours. One hit a brand new and very valuable jig borer, the other detonated as it struck a roof beam. The roof was made of asbestos sheet, which shattered, dissipating the blast upwards. There were no casualties.

At 2 a.m. next day Alfred Townsley was roused by his bedside telephone. Lord Beaverbrook, the Minister of Aircraft Production, himself was on the line demanding full information about the incident and what had been done to ensure continuity of production. He was informed that temporary tool room accommodation was being arranged in a garage at Farlington. The damaged building was in full production again within ten days.

After this raid roof spotters were installed so that personnel were only sent to shelters when bombing was imminent, as too much time was being wasted by sheltering as soon as the sirens sounded. The office block, recently completed, had a central tower which served as the spotters' post. The building was camouflaged by fabric on netting from roof to ground. The next raid, in daylight, was a much more serious affair. As soon as the spotters saw the bombers approaching they sounded the alarm, and with no time to escape by the stairs, slid down the camouflage netting only seconds before the corner of the building was sliced off by a bomb. Several people were killed, but production was not affected.

After test flight and final inspection, aircraft were widely dispersed around the aerodrome to await the Air Transport Auxiliary ferry pilots who delivered them to squadrons. It was discovered on inspecting the aircraft equipment inventory before delivery that some aircraft lacked radio, fire axes and fire extinguishers, although the doors were locked and the dispersals regularly visited by night patrols. Eventually it was discovered that some young boys with evident Commando potential had entered the aerodrome and picked the locks on the aircraft doors. Piles of missing equipment were found in air raid shelters at their homes.

Security was a very serious problem as the aerodrome belonged to Portsmouth Corporation, who took no responsibility for such matters. Control of the site was in the hands of the R.A.F. who, until late 1941, had no personnel there. The access gates, other than the main gates, were wired up with barbed wire but were often broken open during the night. Airspeed made many representations to the Services and the chairman wrote to Lord Beaverbrook after the affair of the child looters.

An admiral was appointed Controller of Aerodrome Defence, so the Board naturally assumed that the problem had been solved. This august figure made two appointments to visit the factory, but did not arrive for either; shortly afterwards he was posted to another command. Within a period of ten days the aerodrome was manned by detachments of the Army, Navy and Royal Air Force at separate times, a splendid example of inter-Service co-operation but not one to give much confidence to Airspeed.

During the war the sirens sounded on average 24 times each month. The factory was straddled by bombs on eight occasions and Alfred Townsley recalled the day when, from his office on the aerodrome side of the works, he could not see the concrete outside the hangars for smoke from incendiary bombs blazing there; not one of them fell on the buildings. The Oxfords were widely dispersed and only four were lost by enemy action.

Based at the factory was an R.A.F. group captain as the Ministry of Aircraft Production overseer. After one of the Oxfords had been destroyed he sent for Townsley, and with asperity, demanded to know why it had been parked with ammunition on board. Townsley laughed at him and said "Do you really think we are as stupid as that?"

"Look here," said the Groupie, bristling at this affront to his authority, "I'm not a damn fool. I saw it burn, and so did you but you won't admit it."

"Right," said Townsley. "Let your report go in, the enquiry can then be opened."

Later the officer had to admit that he did not realise how much magnesium alloy was used in the Oxford, and that he had never seen this particular metal on fire before.

The Lord Mayor of Portsmouth and the Commander-in-Chief, Portsmouth, asked Airspeed if they could send up an aeroplane after each raid to plot the position of bombs which fell into the mud flats around Langstone Harbour. At low tide Townsley and Bob Milne would fly over and plot new craters. It was a rather imprecise exercise, as many bombs fell into the mud without exploding, as was discovered one Sunday morning in 1946 when one went off near the Eastern Road which runs between the aerodrome and the harbour.

Townsley marvelled at the incredible good fortune of this front-line and very important factory which, after the war, was found to be marked on Luftwaffe target maps. The shadow factory at Christchurch was equally fortunate, for in several raids bombs hit the buildings without detonating and nobody was injured.

Many casualties among personnel occurred when their homes were hit in the raids. After one raid Townsley had a telephone call from a very agitated senior executive announcing that a parachute mine was swinging from a tree in his garden. Townsley's advice was "Bolt, as quick as you can". In due course the bomb disposal team defused the offending monster, which could have flattened every house for a mile around.

Two tragedies hit Airspeed in the early stage of the war. Tom Laing, one of the first employees at York, was killed when his car hit a railway bridge during a late-night drive back to Portsmouth after a long journey visiting suppliers, presumably because he fell asleep at the wheel. Flight Lieutenant Cyril Colman, who had carried so much of the responsibility for test and demonstration flying, returned to the R.A.F. on the outbreak of war, was shot up when flying a Beaufighter over Northern France and crashed into the sea when attempting to fly back across the Channel.

The factories were remarkably free of serious accidents, though a Portsmouth sheet metal worker was killed by the explosion when he attempted to weld a fuel tank which had not been purged of fuel vapour. Another man received a broken spine when an Oxford undercarriage leg was retracted, the wing crushing him as it fell; he died two years later.

During the whole of the company's history not one member of the staff was injured in an Airspeed aeroplane other than the two involved in the Courier "hi-jacking" in 1936.

CHAPTER SIX

Horsa

U NTIL 1940 Airspeed's only experience with gliders had been the development of the Tern in 1931, at a time when the Germans were using gliders for pilot training as a way of circumventing the restrictions imposed by the Treaty of Versailles. The German High Command quickly realised that gliders also had a military potential. When Hitler was planning the invasion of Holland and Belgium he met Hanna Reitsch, a well known sporting pilot, who pointed out to him that gliders were quite silent. Realising that the Belgian anti-aircraft defences relied upon sound location equipment, Hitler saw that a major objective, the capture of three vital river bridges, could most easily be achieved by an assault force transported by gliders.

The success of the airborne assault, employing both glider-borne and parachute troops dropped from Junkers Ju 52 transports, upon the bridges over the Albert Canal and Fort Eben Email is well known, yet the Allies showed little interest in airborne forces until June 1940, when Winston Churchill sent a

Horsa gliders at R.A.F. Netheravon in 1945.   *Aeroplane Monthly*

Minute to the Combined Chiefs of Staff requesting that an airborne force be created. Not until the end of 1941 was it decided to form the 1st Airborne Division and to send a detachment of men to Ringway Aerodrome, near Manchester, to carry out trials with parachutes and gliders. The country was scoured for small private gliders, which were towed into the air by hurriedly converted Tiger Moth trainers. The techniques were pioneered in this primitive way by a dedicated body of Army and R.A.F. men led by a Royal Engineer, Lieutenant Colonel John Rock, who was responsible for the formulation of operational policies and future glider requirement specifications.

General Aircraft Company were instructed to tender for a glider to carry eight men. This was the Hotspur, an attractive looking aircraft, but too small for operational use. It was, however, a very effective trainer towed behind Miles Master tugs.

In September 1940, Hessell Tiltman had attended a meeting with Air Vice Marshal Tedder and Dr Roxbee Cox to discuss, among other matters, a projected Airspeed A.S.48 wooden fighter. It was minuted that Dr Cox had suggested to Tedder that Airspeed be instructed to prepare a design for a glider to carry between 24 and 36 fully armed troops. Tiltman indicated that Airspeed would be interested in submitting proposals as soon as a specification was issued, and that in the meantime he would report to his Board and consider the general problems of such an aircraft.

In June 1940, Swan Hunter and Wigham Richardson had sold their shareholding in Airspeed to de Havilland, and four de Havilland directors joined the Board. A. S. Butler became chairman, the other three being F. T. Hearle, W. E. Nixon and F. E. N. St. Barbe. The new Board was dismayed that Tiltman had accepted such a proposition, which seemed to be at the crude end of the aeronautical spectrum.

Hessell retorted "When the Ministry wants you to build an aeroplane to wage war you do it and not mess about!" This probably sowed the seeds of dissension which led to an uneasy and not entirely happy relationship between Tiltman and the de Havilland men, who probably felt a little piqued that two fairly junior de Havilland designers should have started this small firm and have developed the Oxford, which the Ministry instructed D. H. to build at Hatfield. Tiltman, to the day he died, was convinced that this caused resentment and ultimately led to his resignation in 1942. It may, perhaps, be significant that de Havilland appointed Arthur Hagg, who had been their chief designer and was running his own boatbuilding company at Shepperton, to follow Tiltman as technical director and chief designer.

Specification X26/40 was delivered to the Airspeed design office in December 1940. After the takeover, the design office had been moved to Hatfield, where it was destroyed in the bombing raid in October 1940, the staff then being transferred to Salisbury Hall, near London Colney, where the Mosquito was designed and built.

Portsmouth was charged with producing working drawings with the overriding requirement that the components of the glider must be capable of production on machines in normal use in the furniture industry, which would provide the main contractors. Assembly and test flying would be done at R.A.F. Maintenance Units, so a high degree of accuracy was necessary to ensure satisfactory and swift assembly.

The production of the Horsa, as the glider was named, was a triumph of organisation and improvisation in utilising a labour force which was not heavily

The Horsa glider, showing how it was broken down into sub-assemblies for production.

Aeroplane Monthly

committed by wartime needs. Sub-contractors appointed throughout the country included Morris Motors at Cowley, Austin Motors at Longbridge, Wolseley Cars, the London and North Eastern Railway carriage works at York and Doncaster and the L.M.S. carriage works at Wolverton. The shopfitting trade was brought in, George Parnall at Bristol, Frederick Sage at Enfield, and Courtney Pope at Tottenham being among the firms appointed. The Gramophone Company at Hayes and the Metal Box Company at Perivale were in the London group with Hoopers, the Royal coach builders at Acton, Waring and Gillow, and the famous furniture company Harris Lebus, who were consulted at a very early stage in the design of the Horsa. Harris Lebus himself, with his immense knowledge of the trade, was almost an honorary member of the design team. All these major firms and many small ones were involved.

It is unlikely that any other aircraft had a higher percentage of timber in its structure. Even the control column and wheel were of wood. As it was conceived as a single-trip, expendable machine, plain bearings were used on all the controls, which made piloting the Horsa hard work.

Design and construction of the first prototype, DG.597, was carried out in the remarkably short time of ten months. The first two gliders were built at

Salisbury Hall, and a further five at Portsmouth so that military vehicle loading trials could be carried out. It was intended to equip the Mark I Horsa with an explosive cord around the rear fuselage so that it could be quickly jettisoned after landing for rapid disembarkation, the control wires being cut by a pair of powerful wire cutters. Experiments carried out on the fuselage of the second prototype of the abandoned Fleet Shadower reconnaissance machine were not completely successful and on the Mk I Horsa the rear fuselage had to be unbolted from inside, not a very satisfactory arrangement in the heat of battle when seconds counted. The Mark II was developed with a hinged nose and unloading ramp.

The success of the glider was undoubtedly due to the immense care taken at the design stage. The absence of engines necessitated a long nose, so the leading edge of the wing was swept back to give a centre of gravity position which allowed a wide range of loads, from troops to Bailey bridge sections. Streamlining was not of great importance. Although the aerodynamic form was good, it was marred by the blunt nose which was essential to give a good view for the pilots sitting side by side.

A thick high-lift wing section was specified, the wing being built in three parts, centre section and outer panels. The deep single main spar was built of laminated spruce booms joined by laminated posts at intervals. The leading edge was formed into a D-section torsion box with a pre-formed plywood skin fixed to the upper and lower surfaces of the boom. Very large flaps were located at the trailing edge of the centre section and on the outer panels between the ailerons. The flaps were operated by pneumatic rams, as was the undercarriage

The prototype A.S.51 Horsa, DG.597. *Aeroplane Monthly*

jettison gear and main wheel brakes. The jettison gear was most ingenious, allowing the release of the top oleo leg fixings by means of the pilot's control. As the complete assembly dropped downwards, hingeing about the main Vee struts, the wheels collided with each other and caused an unhingeing moment which released the Vee struts. If the release was carried out too early there was a serious risk of the undercarriage bouncing off the ground and hitting the Horsa.

Large flaps were essential as a very steep landing approach was necessary to give the shortest possible exposure to fire from the ground. The maximum "down" angle was 80 degrees, but to give maximum lift they were depressed 45 degrees. The tail unit was similar in construction to the wing.

The fuselage was a wooden semi-monocoque in three sections bolted together. The nose was the complete cockpit assembly, the centre a straight circular barrel and the tail section tapered to the rudder post. The centre fuselage was built on four main longerons located on laminated ply covered frames. A stout floor was built with transverse members faced with plywood, substantial floor members transmitting the loads involved in transporting heavy military equipment and the landing loads from the laminated ash skids beneath the fuselage. The whole assembly was covered with diagonally applied plywood skins.

The aileron controls were linked at the wing joints by what became known as "buffer boxes", a system of butting plates developed in 1931 for the tiny Tern glider and in 1933 for the Courier.

A mock-up was quickly constructed at Salisbury Hall. This led to some embarrassment when the analysis of technical requirements led to workmen and inspectors being accosted by a draughtsman brandishing a jam jar with a demand that they should relieve themselves into it. When they recovered from this affront to their dignity they were informed that it was necessary to provide appropriate comforts for the troops and, as the container must be as small as possible to save space and weight, an average volume per man must be determined. Surprisingly, no-one seems to have thought, initially, that these private needs could have been met by straight jettison out of the fuselage, relying upon air dispersal to avoid offence below. Eventually a tube was installed and further ruffled feelings avoided.

The necessity of conserving steel led to the use of old Portsmouth Corporation gas lamp standards as bases for building jigs, whilst Morrison-type air raid shelters with flat tops were used to lay out components for assembly.

The test flights of the prototype at Fairey's Great West Road aerodrome, now part of London Airport, were carried out under rather primitive conditions. The only hangar available was a Bellman type, a series of curved trusses running from ground level at either side, clad with corrugated sheeting. It was only 100 feet (30.48m) wide at the base, with vertical braced girders 5 feet (1.5m) in from each side. As the Horsa was 88 feet (26.82m) in span the wing tip clearance was

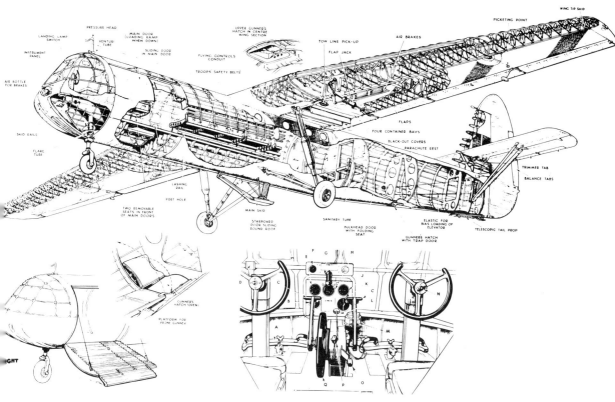

Cutaway drawing of the Horsa Mk.I. *Flight*

minimal. To make life easier for the handling crew the very enterprising erection foreman decided to remove these girders, which were hurriedly replaced when it became clear that the Horsa was likely to be enveloped by the collapsing hangar.

On a cold September night the Horsa fell off one of its rigging jacks, which penetrated the fuselage. The first flight was due next morning, so a rush repair job was carried out whilst men scoured the site for electric fires to dry out the glue and dope. These were connected and switched on. The whole aerodrome was plunged into darkness as the main fuses blew, but the glider was ready on time.

Mr McFarlane, the Air Ministry Resident Technical Officer at Portsmouth, had delegated to the A.I.D. at Fairey's factory the responsibility of supervising the first flight on 12th September 1941. Just before take-off it was discovered that the vital paperwork was not in the hands of Fairey's Chief A.I.D. Inspector, but was still in McFarlane's office. John Jupp, the works manager, was called to the A.I.D. office and told in the sternest tones that without the paperwork the flight could certainly not take place. Jupp was delighted to hear the Whitley tug's engine note rise to take-off revs, and as he looked out of the window the bomber was half way across the aerodrome and the Horsa beginning to move away from the far hedge. It was quickly airborne with George Errington holding it down to avoid lifting the Whitley's tail.

As pilot of the Whitley towing aircraft, Flight Lieutenant R. W. H. Carter was deeply involved in the development flying of the Horsa. A Royal New Zealand Air Force officer, he had, as a small boy, become extremely interested in Airspeed aeroplanes, which were the subject of Press comment in his home country. He spent many hours making models of the Envoy and Courier. In July 1941, he was posted from Farnborough, where he had been flying the General Aircraft Hotspur training glider, to assist with the trials of the Horsa at Portsmouth and Great West Road. The excitement of towing a large glider into the air was quite overshadowed by the thrill of seeing a Courier in the hangar at Portsmouth. Although he had flown most of the latest types at Farnborough the

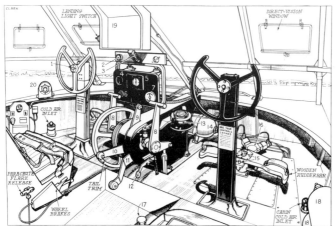

The cockpit of the Horsa. All the controls had plain bearings, which made piloting the Horsa hard work.

Aeroplane Monthly

Courier was the one he really wanted to fly to recapture the pleasures of his boyhood. This was soon arranged.

Nick Carter attended mock-up conferences at the Harris Lebus factory and, whilst waiting for the final assembly of the prototype, prepared the Whitley which he was to fly. It was stripped of turrets, armour plating, bomb racks and all operational equipment.

Carter recalls: "We carried out the first towed taxi trials of the prototype Horsa, DG.597, piloted by George Errington, on the old grass aerodrome at Heathrow in August 1941. From slow runs we gradually worked up to take-off speed, with the Horsa releasing and the Whitley continuing to take off, shedding the tow rope and doing a circuit. This procedure was repeated many times. On one occasion the tow release on the Whitley jammed so that we trailed the rope through the barbed wire on the aerodrome boundary taking a length of it with us. We eventually landed, Whitley, tow rope and wire all together. After disentanglement the fence was returned to its rightful place by our tractor.

"The flights which followed, during September 1941, were full of interest and excitement. We were frequently visited by Chiefs of Staff, Ministry of Aircraft Production officials, senior officers of the U.S. forces and others. There was also a good deal of interest by Winston Churchill himself. There were numerous hold-ups for modifications to the Horsa, the towing assemblies and because of bad weather. We would fly at any time of the day on any day of the week, it was a question of putting in flying time whenever we could.

"We were flying late one evening when I judged from the Whitley fuel gauges that I could make one more flight before packing up. We ran out of fuel at around 3,000 feet with the Horsa still on tow, thick London haze and mist below and not sure of our exact position. As George Errington cast off in the Horsa his final words over the inter-com were 'See you in Hyde Park!' It was pure luck that we both found the airfield again and got down intact, the Whitley showing the Horsa how it too could execute steep gliding turns. We never again relied upon our fuel gauges but dipped the tanks when the fuel was low. During these early flights we deliberately kept fuel loads down and re-fuelling was a rather frequent business.

"The Merlin engines took a real hammering with so much maximum power operation at high temperatures, and only once during the whole series of trials were new engines required. The Whitley was often pulled violently about the sky during the handling trials but not once did we break a tow rope.

"One cannot recall those days without being reminded of the wonderful spirit of all those involved in the Horsa project. What a grand bunch they were. Completely dedicated to their work, toiling long hours, often frustrated by the whims and moans of the pilots and others, yet never once did they fail to give their maximum effort.

"By the end of November 1941, we had completed a wide range of handling trials under various loadings, high tow, low tow, using various towing bridles and attachments and different length ropes. Not only were these flights to prove the capability of the Horsa, they were used to form the basis of a heavy glider towing technique from which was evolved the method of operation under active service conditions.

"An amusing incident occurred during a take-off at Heathrow using the longest tow rope of all. The Horsa went a little too high and, when eased down, caused the rope to sag in a huge bow which scraped across the telephone wires along the Great West Road producing a loud scream audible to those on the ground a considerable distance away. I have often wondered what noises were produced at the local telephone exchange.

"For full load tests on grass we moved to Baginton, near Coventry, where we had a longer take-off run. Nearby Honiley was used for the hard runway tests. During November and December numerous flights were made, first with the Horsa at full load in ballast and then with the Whitley ballasted as well. We flew the combination many times at maximum combined weight. The late autumn and early winter weather in the Midlands was not exactly ideal for our purpose and there were many delays on this account. One day when visibility suddenly dropped to zero we decided to take an early lunch and set off in two cars, one following the other straight across the airfield, to the entrance gate on the far side. We lost the leading car in the fog, then collided with it with a hefty thud about ten minutes later whilst still trying to find our way out.

"On one fully loaded flight with the Horsa we were wallowing laboriously upward with throttles wide open when we unexpectedly and unintentionally entered the cloud base. George Errington afterwards admitted that this was the worst experience of his career; at first he was able to follow the tunnel-like vortices of the Whitley's propellers but then lost contact and fell far below the tug. I had to use all my strength and both hands to hold the control column forward and prevent a disastrous stall. For a moment I wondered if George had forsaken the controls for the Elsan. It was the resulting loss of height which brought us below the cloud base again, on an even keel with much perspiration on our brows. We were very lucky to get away with nothing worse than fright.

"On another occasion at Netheravon one of the jettisonable undercarriage units failed to jettison on a full load test. The observers were not amused when I ordered them to dump three tons of concrete ballast so that we could again try for a safe landing along the hillside, a manoeuvre which was entirely successful. Yet another jettisoned undercarriage bounced up so high that it hit the tailplane removing a large part of that useful component. The flight path was decidedly in the nature of a switchback but we returned safely. Undercarriages certainly gave us problems. One failed to release at the appointed moment, later falling into a garden where the family were being photographed on the lawn by the son. The assembly hurtled to earth just between the photographer and his subject. I have often pondered upon the expressions which that camera recorded. Another stuck leg fell into an Army Camp, the Army, thinking that it was a new type of bomb, wired off the area and sent for the long suffering bomb disposal squad.

"We flew the second prototype Horsa, DG 600, in January 1942, taking it up to Snaith, in Yorkshire, for a series of tests. The first machine to be handed over to the Airborne Forces Experimental Establishment was delivered to Ringway in February and we heard later that it had been landed unceremoniously on a hangar roof by none other than Robert Kronfeld, the famous sailplane pilot. In mid-February we flew the first Christchurch assembled Horsa, DG.604, out of the small grass field there, and continued development flying with the first machine, DG.597, which had been undergoing extensive modifications.

"When the time came to use the Handley Page Halifax as a tug for the extended trials we received one of the prototypes which had done most of the flying during the development of the type at Radlett and in the R.A.F.

acceptance trials. We spent a lot of time trying to make this machine serviceable at Portsmouth. During one of the many check flights I did on it we had the unpleasant experience of the rudders overbalancing and firmly locking fully over after an engine failure. We entertained the locals with an uncontrollable falling leaf act over Langstone Harbour. With the frantic help of my flight engineer, we managed somehow to get the brute back on Portsmouth Airport. We thereafter made such loud and rude noises in the right places that we were immediately allocated a brand new Halifax straight off the production lines at Radlett.

"We did our first Halifax tow at Baginton at the end of February using the first prototype which was then handed over to A.F.E.E. Ringway in early March.

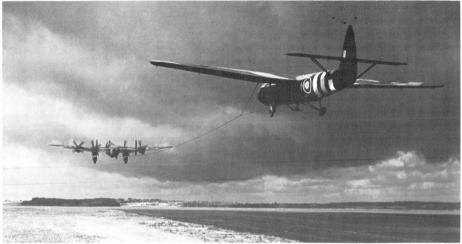

A Horsa taking off behind a Halifax Mk.III. "Invasion stripes" can be seen around the rear fuselage.   *Aeroplane Monthly*

Then followed production testing of the Horsas beginning to come off the production line at Christchurch and the preliminary inspection of Netheravon as a possible base for a series of Halifax/Horsa development tests.

"The very limited take-off run at Christchurch was causing us some concern. There was a maximum of 800 yards, boundary to boundary, with oak and fir trees at one end and bungalows at the other. We were forced to use a shortened tow rope and were unable to get the combination out of the airfield in a cross wind. Repeated requests to have, at least, some of the trees removed fell on deaf ears, so we finally refused to tow any more Horsas out of Christchurch until something was done. That caused much panic in high places and immediate action followed. Enough trees were removed to give us a few more valuable feet for take-off, rope dropping and landing the Whitley. There were many hair raising incidents with visiting aircraft overshooting when attempting to land.

"In March 1942, I went to General Aircraft for the flight trials of the giant Hamilcar tank-carrying glider, returning to Airspeed in November and taking up permanent residence at Christchurch. Horsa production was now well under way, Oxfords were coming off the lines in large numbers and we were kept fairly busy with experimental flying. George Errington, Bob Milne and Ron Clear used to take it in turns to come over from Portsmouth when more than one pilot was required. We paid regular visits to R.A.F. Brize Norton and the Maintenance Unit at Cosford to check-fly the Horsas being assembled there.

The General Aircraft Hamilcar glider disgorging a T-19 Locust tank.

Aeroplane Monthly

"It was at Brize Norton, whilst testing a new machine, that I had my first experience of being jettisoned by the tug on take-off after an engine failure. The only available emergency landing area was a small field away to my left. It was already occupied by cows but we managed to touch down between them with the wings passing over them. Most of the animals went on feeding after only a casual glance at the intruder.

"After flight test we usually dropped the gliders into either Netheravon, Wroughton or Hurn for handing over to the Airborne Forces. One day, after such a trip to Brize Norton, George decided that he would like to fly the Whitley back to Christchurch and proceeded to carry out some blind flying practice in cloud on the way. The wind at around 3000 feet was very much stronger than had been forecast and, when we broke cloud expecting to see Christchurch below us we discovered to our horror that we were in the midst of the Southampton balloon barrage! We were hemmed in by them and flew on over the water as George calmly picked his way between them, a very frightening experience.

"His only comment was 'We shall have to warn Balloon Command about this and tell them to put another balloon in the corridor, it is most dangerous, we could easily have been a Hun'.

"Horsa production was top priority and weather conditions at Christchurch often made it extremely difficult to clear each week's output on time. Situated right on the coast, we were frequently held up during the summer by sea mist creeping in and blanketing the airfield. There was often a last minute panic on the Friday and Saturday to clear the week's quota.

"By now we were doing a lot of flying from Netheravon using the Halifax tug. We flew the Mark II Horsa with the hinged nose, doing undercarriage jettison tests and skid landings under all load conditions.

"At times we had more Horsas at Christchurch than we could cope with, many awaited delivery and others first flight or check tests. We became quite expert at landing a Horsa so that it came to rest just where it was required, either back on the tarmac in front of the flight shed or alongside and in line with others at the side of the airfield. On more than one occasion we rolled right up to the flight shed doors. We had a violent storm one day with wind gusting up to 92 m.p.h. and tearing many of the Horsas from their moorings, carrying them into the air and piling them up against one another or against the factory buildings. One became airborne and flew past the pilots' office, dangling its anchors of five-gallon oil drums full of concrete only inches from our windows. Another, which was parked close to the trees on the edge of the airfield, was lifted bodily upwards, executed a perfect half loop on to its back and crashed upside down on to fir trees, stripping off the branches and leaving only the trunks, minus the bark, sticking up through the wings and fuselage. We took photographs of this one and later framed them with the caption 'It's all right, old boy, she really can do steep turns at the stall, the designer said so!' Mounted on the wall in the pilots' office, it always caused much interest and amusement and was, in time, appreciated by the designers themselves.

"The last of the Oxfords coincided with the increased production of the Horsa, which continued to the autumn of 1945, by which time de Havilland Mosquito production was also under way. Mossie and Horsa flying continued until 1946 when I left the company. My long and very pleasant association with it came to an end and I returned to New Zealand in 1947 to find my old model of the Courier still prominently displayed in my home. The wheel had turned full circle."

Bob Milne remembers an occasion when he and George Errington had carried out stability trials at Netheravon and were bringing the Horsa back to Christchurch. Just beyond Winchester the Halifax release gear was inadvertently operated, leaving Milne and his observer in free flight with the tug disappearing in the distance. Bob landed in a large field well staked with massive poles expressly arranged to prevent such incursions, as was the custom in the 1940's. Miraculously he dodged them all. The landowner was exercising his dog nearby and drove Milne to the nearest telephone.

In no time four police cars were on the scene, the Horsa crew was arrested and quickly driven to an underground police station at Winchester where they were grilled for several hours. Bob Milne quite reasonably suggested to the chief inspector that Airspeeds should be telephoned to corroborate his story, but this was far too logical for the policemen who were really enjoying their brief moment of military glory. In any case security officials were coming from London. Later developments were sheer farce.

Milne and the observer were taken to the Horsa to remove the secret equipment. A platoon of the Welsh Fusiliers was in occupation and had fenced off the glider and erected a small guard room at the entrance, where the crew were forbidden to enter.

After much argument and delay the guard N.C.O. was persuaded to contact his unit by telephone. The unit Commanding Officer phoned his Command H.Q., who, in turn, approached the War Office. The War Office took the matter up with the Security Forces, who released the crew in time for lunch at Portsmouth on the following day. Two days later, George Errington towed the Horsa back to Portsmouth after an incident which must rank high in the annals of bumbling official idiocy.

Shortly after this episode a test series began at R.A.F. Thorney Island, near Chichester. This station was in constant use by fighter aircraft returning damaged from ops and the runway could only be made available to the Horsas for very short periods. The Resident Technical Officer in charge of the tests had a rather irrational dislike of the Horsa and refused to fly in it.

One morning the Halifax and Horsa were ranged at the end of the runway, awaiting the paperwork authorising the flight. The engine temperatures were rising when the R.T.O.'s small camouflaged car was seen rushing round the perimeter track. He leapt out with the papers and was unceremoniously bundled into the Horsa as the Halifax moved off. As the tow rope stretched to its full length and the glider moved off with a jerk, the luckless R.T.O. was thrown off his feet and hurled to the tail. After a 35-minute flight, his mood was not improved by finding that the Station Commander had impounded his car which had been left at the end of the runway.

Testing Oxfords and Horsas on the South Coast was a rather nerve-racking affair in the early days of the war as the Luftwaffe probed the defences. Encounters with enemy aircraft were frequent and the absence of armament led to many frustrating situations for the test pilots.

Ron Clear had several quaint experiences whilst testing Horsas. Flying a Halifax, he was towing one flown by George Errington who had instructed that, although oxygen equipment was not installed in the glider, he should be towed to the maximum possible height. Over Salisbury the aircraft were at 16,000 feet (4,877m) and still climbing when Ron, watching his rear view mirror, saw the Horsa wallowing a little. As the intercom cable in the tow rope was unserviceable no verbal communication between the pilots was possible, but suddenly a white handkerchief appeared out of the Horsa's direct vision window and the glider released. Ron flew back to base to await the return of George from his landing site by whatever means of transport he could commandeer. After parking the

A Horsa ready for take-off from a glider conversion unit where pilots learnt to handle these aircraft. This photograph was issued in September, 1943, as preparations were made for the invasion of Europe.   *Aeroplane Monthly*

Halifax he was amazed to see George's Horsa appear, circle the aerodrome and make a perfect landing. He walked out to meet Errington, who gave him a most perfunctory greeting, saying nothing about the occurrence. Significantly, the Horsa was equipped with oxygen before the next flight.

In 1941 the War Cabinet was becoming increasingly concerned by the potential threat of the German battleship *Tirpitz*. With her sister ships she was able to pin down a large proportion of the British Fleet in the North Sea, her mere presence in port presenting a fearsome hazard to our Atlantic convoys, so vulnerable to raiding forays by powerful heavily armed ships. It was decided that bombing attacks on *Tirpitz* in the Norwegian fiords were essential. Only Barnes Wallis's 12,000 lb (5,443 kg) bomb was capable of penetrating the massive deck armour of the vessel. Handley Page, Shorts and A. V. Roe dismissed suggestions that the Halifax, Stirling or Lancaster could be modified to carry this huge bomb.

A desperate situation required a desperate remedy. Airspeed was asked to consider converting the Horsa to carry the weapon. Such an operation could only be a suicide mission for the crews of the Horsa and the tug, both of whom would have to fly slowly, in a straight line, over one of the heaviest concentrations of anti-aircraft fire ever concentrated in one ship.

The A.S.52 Horsa I bomber conversion was designed to Specification X3/41. A large cut-out in the underside of the fuselage allowed the bomb to fall freely with a minimum drag penalty in flight. A prototype was flown in 1941.

Roy Chadwick, the brilliant designer of the Lancaster, was not one to admit defeat and continued to work on the possibility of the Lancaster being converted to carry "Tallboy," as the bomb was known. His success led to the sinking of

Tirpitz by a force of 29 Lancasters on 12th November 1944, so the Airspeed "glider bomber" was abandoned.

The introduction of the Horsa into large-scale operational service brought many problems of towing aircraft availability, and in 1942 the Airborne Forces were in danger from inter-Service rivalry. Bomber Command C-in-C Air Marshal "Bomber" Harris took the view that aircraft would be much better employed in his own strategic bombing offensive than in glider towing and carrying parachutists.

Churchill thought the increasing production of the American C.47 Dakota would ultimately provide all the paratrooping facilities needed, and was worried by the massive production programme for Horsas which, having to be parked in the open air, would deteriorate before they were ready for operations. There is no evidence, however, to indicate that the cuts he ordered were implemented.

The first operational task in which the Horsa was involved was an attack on the Norwegian heavy water plant near Rjukan, an almost impossibly difficult target in a deep afforested valley with 3,000 foot (914m) walls overlooked by a 5,000 foot (1,520m) mountain. The heavy water plant, essential to the Germans who were believed to be carrying out research on atom bomb development, was located on a rock plateau 1,000 feet (305m) above the river, a precipitous slope

Loading a jeep into a Horsa Mk.II. *Aeroplane Monthly*

above the plant making all forms of assault extremely difficult and hazardous. Two Horsas towed by Halifaxes and crewed by volunteers from the Royal Engineers took off on the night of 19th November 1942. The first pair flew into icing conditions over Norway and the tow rope broke, the glider crashing into the mountains, killing eight of the seventeen men on board. The survivors were either poisoned by a German doctor or executed by the Gestapo. The other pair crashed into the mountains, the few survivors being shot by Hitler's order.

The prelude to the next operation, an attack on Sicily, was an epic flight by Horsas and Halifaxes from Britain to North Africa. Only three of the original 30 Horsas were lost during the flight, which took them within 100 miles (160 km) of Luftwaffe bases in southwest France. The operation itself was less successful, only 12 of the 140 gliders, Horsas and American Waco Hadrians, reaching the target. No fewer than 47 landed in the sea, partly due to the reluctance of American tug pilots to approach the beach nearer than 3,000 yards (2,743m) and also to the pilots' failure to realise that air over the sea cools very rapidly after sundown; all the training undertaken by the glider pilots had been over land.

In 1944 three Horsas were involved in a memorable flight after lying abandoned on a Tunisian airstrip for the six months following the invasion of

Horsas marshalled on an Italian airfield before the Allied landings in Southern France, 1944.
Aeroplane Monthly

Sicily exposed to the ravages of searing heat, wind, rain, sand and Arabs. Three C.47s flew crews into the airstrip. Not a man was capable of carrying out a full inspection of the derelicts, so they checked the controls, uttered a prayer and pressed on, hoping for the best. The Horsas were flown 250 miles (402 km) across the Mediterranean to Comiso where they were filled with anything which would constitute a load of 7,000 lb (3,175 kg). No loading charts were available to check the position of the centre of gravity, so the time-honoured method of hanging on the tail and checking that the nose wheel could be made to leave the ground was employed. Then followed a hazardous flight to Bari in Italy, with the aircraft barely clearing the hills in heavy snow and gale force winds.

At Bari they were briefed to land a Russian military mission to General Tito's partisan headquarters in Yugoslavia. The operation was ultimately carried out by U.S. Hadrians, the crews of the American C.47s declaring that their aircraft were incapable of towing the Horsas over the Dinaria Alps. So the trusty Horsas were ignominiously dumped.

The pilots of a Horsa at the controls. *Aeroplane Monthly*

The invasion of Europe in 1944 brought major and awesome responsibilities to the 6th Airborne Division and Horsas played a major role in the operations which are described in detail in *Winged Pegasus* by Lieutenant-Colonel George Chatterton, commanding officer of the 1st Battalion, the Glider Pilot Regiment and a pioneer of airborne warfare.

Planning the landing sites began in February 1944, on the premise that landings would be made at night on the flat, treeless land around Caen. This plan was quickly abandoned as the potential landing zones began to sprout massive poles 20 feet (6m) high and 1½ feet (.5m) in diameter. Training went ahead to ensure the highest degree of operational efficiency in landing a large number of gliders in a small area in the shortest possible time. In March 1944, a spectacular success was achieved at Wellford, Berkshire when 97 gliders were towed off, flown a considerable distance and all landed back at the airfield on a marker at the planned ten-second intervals.

In the training programme only three fatal accidents occurred in operations ranging from single flights to major exercises involving more than 100 gliders in each, a remarkable tribute to the skill of members of the Glider Pilot Regiment. There were certainly some hair-raising experiences. One rather inexperienced pilot was so buffeted by the slipstream of the tug that the Horsa turned on to its back and flew inverted for some miles to gain height before rolling back on to an even keel. Another Horsa, on tow behind a Halifax, flew into cloud and emerged some minutes later. To the pilot's dismay the towrope followed closely the surface of the windscreen, disappearing above and behind them where the Halifax pilot was desperately trying to control his aircraft, the tail of which was being pulled down by the glider, which had overtaken the tug in cloud.

The success of the rehearsals for the Operation Overlord invasion had quelled most of the doubts about the potentialities of glider operations held by many senior officers, and the Royal Aircraft Establishment at Farnborough organised a Development Flight under the command of Wing Commander T. Morrison to evaluate all aspects of glider performance and operational techniques. It was this Flight which initiated the work on the loading problems of the Horsa Mk I which led to the development of the Mark II with a hinged nose.

Methods of towing were investigated. One of the more terrifying experiments used two single-engine Miles Master tugs, normally used to tow the small Hotspur training glider. The tow ropes from the aircraft passed through a pulley on the nose of the Horsa. Take-off was particularly alarming as the Mercury radial engines of the Master were heavily overloaded and had a reputation for failure on take-off. Spitfires and Beaufighters were also used as tugs. The Spitfire was too much of a thoroughbred to accept this indignity with good grace and responded most violently to the presence of such a load behind it. Towing a fully loaded Horsa behind a Wellington also produced problems.

The controls became extremely stiff and inspection revealed that the geodetic construction of the machine, a form of metal 'trellis work', had elongated appreciably with the drag of the glider.

A very important aspect of the work of the Flight was the use of tail parachutes to steepen the descent of the gliders. A Horsa pilot could achieve a very steep diving approach at 100 m.p.h. (161 km/hr), pull out at 50 feet and deploy the parachute to arrive at ground level at a reasonable landing speed in the shortest possible time. The technique was immensely valuable in approaching landing zones defended by small arms fire, but great skill and iron nerves were demanded of the pilot.

In the preliminary stages of Operation Overlord a spectacular success was achieved in the capture of the Merville battery. Two Horsas landed in darkness, one a quarter of a mile (400m) and the other 50 yards (46m) from the guns, which were soon silenced. The pilots, Staff Sgts Bone and Kerr, were awarded the Distinguished Flying Medal for their extraordinary courage and skill.

After three preliminary actions the major D Day landings were made by 68 Horsas carrying men of the 6th Airborne Division, with four giant Hamilcars carrying heavy equipment. Of these, 47 Horsas and two Hamilcars reached the landing zone, where strong cross-winds caused a number of collisions. Later on D Day a landing by 250 gliders, mostly Horsas, delivered 7,500 men into the battle in daylight.

No account of the Horsa's operational career would be complete without reference to the tragedy of Arnhem. The bridge at this Dutch town was a critical factor in breaching a defence line which the retreating enemy had established in

The towing arrangements of a Horsa.
via Aeroplane Monthly

Holland, and its capture would have enabled the Allies to thrust northward out-flanking the Siegfried Line and cutting off the Germans in Holland. It was clear, however, that an airborne assault there, 60 miles (96 km) inside enemy territory, would require rapid reinforcement to achieve success.

A combination of unsatisfactory landing zones up to eight miles (13 km) from the bridge, a failure of radio communication and the rank misfortune that, unknown to Intelligence, a Panzer Division was resting in the area conspired to defeat the valiant efforts of the Airborne Forces. Four days of immense heroism could not prevail against the rapid build-up of enemy forces, and withdrawal became essential. The final toll of the Glider Pilot Regiment was 23 officers and 124 other ranks killed, with 31 officers and 438 other ranks taken prisoner. During those days of battle 660 glider landings brought in 4,500 men, 95 guns and 544 jeeps or larger vehicles, a remarkable achievement, superbly executed and deserving of success.

The next Horsa operation was the capture of a bridge over the River Isel, a tributary of the Rhine, and of the village of Hammenkeln, in which enemy troops were billeted. On 24th March 1945, no fewer than 440 gliders were towed off, only four of which aborted the mission due to broken tow ropes or tug engine failure. The Mark II Horsa with its hinged nose and landing ramp was now in large-scale service. This made a major contribution to the success of the landing, carried out in the face of heavy enemy fire. Nine out of ten of the troop-carrying gliders landed as planned, but only 88 of them were undamaged, most of the others being hit by light flak and small arms fire, and 37 were burnt

A Horsa survivor had a miraculous escape when flying in with a jeep and trailer full of explosives. At 1,000 feet (305m) flak hit the fuel tank of the jeep, and immediately the Horsa was a mass of flame. With great skill the pilot continued his approach and lowered the flaps. At 50 feet (15m) the flames reached the explosives and the Horsa disintegrated. The survivor, an officer of the 7th Battalion Devonshire Regiment, regained consciousness 30 minutes later in a hay stack, surrounded by wreckage and the bodies of his companions.

The Rhine crossings were the final sorties of the Horsas, although some Mark IIs went to India to take part in operations against the Japanese. The surrender of Japan took place soon afterwards and the Glider Pilot Regiment was posted to Palestine with the 6th Airborne Division and, later, to Aldershot, where its strength was greatly reduced. This fine force which had acquitted itself so gallantly was disbanded and all that is left is a Regimental Association whose President is Brigadier George Chatterton, O.B.E., D.S.O. In February 1976, the Brigadier was quoted in the *Portsmouth Evening News*: "No one else in the world did anything like this, and there could not have been battles like Arnhem without us flying in the troops and the guns. I do not think that many people today realise the part those gliders played in the war. Those Horsas were wonderful things, they took off like birds."

He told the author: "Most of the pilots had volunteered for the Air Force during the Battle of Britain, the Battle ending before they were trained, so they re-mustered for Army service, being given 100 hours flying training at Elementary Flying Training Schools, graduating to Hotspurs and ultimately to Horsas and Hamilcars.

"I was a fully trained fighter pilot before transferring to gliders without any dual instruction. Colonel John Rock, who commanded the Glider Pilot Regiment, was killed in a night landing accident and I took over command. From our strictly professional point of view these gliders were almost a joke, costing £10,000 each and built almost entirely of wood by the furniture

Brigadier George Chatterton, O.B.E. D.S.O.

industry. We left them on the airfields at the mercy of appalling weather for months on end, and they stood up to it magnificently. The only snag with the Horsa I was the problem of unloading it by unbolting the tail section to remove jeeps and six-pounder guns. I had a lot to do with the developments which led to the far more satisfactory Mk II.

"With limited experience, the glider pilots pulled off the most difficult and unusual landings, up to 100 gliders being landed on one zone at intervals of 30 seconds with very few accidents.

"Apart from their incredibly high flying standards, the glider pilots were trained to fight in almost every position in the field. Fifty per cent were casualties and they won 175 decorations, a unique achievement for such a small force."

Brigadier Chatterton was himself responsible for 2,000 gliders deployed in Europe. At the time of the Normandy invasion no less than 7,000 tons of equipment and stores were delivered by glider. He ended his account on a humorous note with the story of one of the Horsas towed from Cornwall to North Africa. The tow rope broke as it was crossing the North African coast and

A Horsa landing at Netheravon, showing the size of the flaps. *Aeroplane Monthly*

a landing was made near a remote native village. A search party eventually found the glider and its crew, a picture of domestic bliss, with chickens, goats and two native girls and the Horsa as a desirable residence!

It has been suggested that the glider warfare concept was very inefficient and wasteful, the gliders being expendable and the pilots trained to fly only a few one-way missions, whilst in training they took up the time of aircrew and aircraft which could have been used on the strategic bombing operations.

Unquestionably, in the early days of the war, the German airborne operations were very successful due to the surprise element and the lack of effective opposition from the ground or the air. The Allied effort in Sicily and Holland almost succeeded, the margin of failure being small but catastrophic. The meticulous planning of an airborne operation, either by parachutists or gliders, can be negated at the moment of landing by slight miscalculations or ill luck. The appalling vulnerability of troops in the landing phase is the Achilles heel of airborne warfare.

If however, an operation such as Arnhem, where success could have shortened the war, had been a triumph of arms, then it could certainly have been argued that cost effectiveness was at an extremely high level. On D Day the performance of the 6th Airborne Division in a difficult night assault can be seen as possibly the finest example of such an operation in the history of warfare.

It remains for future historians to draw up the balance sheet. The only certain conclusion is that the Airborne Forces included some of the best fighting men the world has ever seen and that the Airspeed Horsa glider was a worthy mount in which to exercise their courage and military skills.

Not one Horsa has been preserved. A fuselage may be seen at the Museum of Army Flying at Middle Wallop and the front section of another is in the Mosquito Museum at Salisbury Hall, London Colney, its birthplace. Nothing more remains of this remarkable aircraft.

CHAPTER SEVEN

Ambassador

IN the blackest days of the Second World War the Government set up a committee under the chairmanship of Lord Brabazon of Tara, one of the earliest aviation pioneers, to study the potential shape of civil aviation in Britain after the war and to recommend the types of aircraft to be developed.

Britain, having already agreed with the Americans to concentrate upon bombers whilst they built military transport aircraft, was at a serious disadvantage. Douglas were building vast numbers of C.54 four-engined transports of advanced design requiring little modification to convert to the Skymaster airliner which gave the American airlines such a commanding lead as soon as the war ended. Britain's only "airliners" at that time were the Lancastrian, a converted Lancaster bomber carrying nine passengers, and the York, basically a Lancaster with a new and much larger fuselage capable of carrying 24 passengers in unpressurised and noisy discomfort.

One of the types recommended by the Brabazon Committee was a DC.3/Dakota replacement. The Government invited Airspeed to put forward proposals, within the limitations set out by the Director General of Civil Aviation that work should only proceed in so far as it could be carried out without interfering with war production.

Hessell Tiltman, that talented designer who had been responsible for all the previous Airspeed machines, had become a victim of the 1940 de Havilland takeover. After disagreements with the D. H. Board he resigned to join Marcus Langley in forming the Tiltman-Langley Laboratories at Redhill and was succeeded by A. E. Hagg, who had already worked with Airspeed on the A.S.56 wooden fighter, abandoned after the bombing of the Hatfield drawing office in 1940. His previous airliner experience was mainly with the de Havilland Albatross, a very elegant wooden aircraft which he designed in 1936, and the de Havilland Flamingo, D.H.'s first all-metal machine, development of which was terminated by the war. A special design office was established at Fairmile Manor, near Cobham, Surrey, with a staff which quickly grew to 40.

Hagg was convinced that the thinking behind the direct DC.3 replacement was flawed and that the post-war growth of air transport was under-estimated by the civil aviation authorities, a view which proved to be absolutely correct. He was also convinced that reluctance to accept high cruising speed on the grounds of high operating and maintenance costs was equally unsound, and that good operating economics would inevitably result from high cruising speed if attained by refinement of aerodynamic form.

Low operating cost per passenger mile presupposed two basic premises: one, that direct flying costs must be spread by having the largest number of passengers per crew, and secondly, that the indirect or fixed costs be spread by employing the aircraft at a high rate of utilisation. A fine balance, therefore, must be struck between the number of passengers per service and the number of services per day. A high economical operating speed must inevitably contribute to these requirements by making possible both high overall utilisation and a high revenue carrying capacity per hour.

Hagg succeeded in convincing the Civil Aviation Authority that the DC.3 replacement was a non-starter, and his initial proposals for the new A.S.57 project were for a twin-engined all-metal machine of about 40,000 lb (18,000

The A.S.57 Ambassador, known by British European Airways as the Elizabethan. *British Airways*

kg) all-up weight with provision for a pressure cabin; tricycle undercarriage; cruising speed of 200 m.p.h. (322 km/hr); and good single-engine performance with a payload of 7,000 lb (3,175 kg), including 30 passengers, over a still air distance of 1,000 miles (1,610 km). Spacious quarters for the passengers were still considered to be de rigueur in 1944, doubtless stemming from nostalgia for the comfortable old Short Empire flying boats in the days when airline flying was a pleasure for the passengers. In April Airspeed put forward a 24-seat cabin plan for the B.O.A.C. Empire routes; for shorter-haul European routes 40-seat layouts were being discussed.

The twin-engine layout created much controversy. Four engines for reliability had almost become a cult in airline circles, but Hagg argued that it was fallacious. Provided that the two engines had a sufficiently high power-to-weight ratio to give safe single-engine take-off performance, the advantages must lie with the twin in terms of initial cost, depreciation, fuel costs and weight, to say nothing of the saving in maintenance costs achieved by the reduction in the number of engines and ancillary equipment. From the viewpoint of the airline a fault in one engine means a delay in leaving the ramp; "Why double the risk?" said Arthur Hagg, convincingly.

The unusual high-wing layout evolved logically from a comparison of dimensions with a comparable low-wing design. To give adequate propeller ground clearance with a low wing would require a much longer, and therefore heavier, undercarriage. The cabin floor would then be 11 feet 6 inches (3.5m) from the ground instead of the 3 feet 6 inches (1.05m) of the high-wing aircraft. Additional advantages were the continuous area of lift from the upper surface of the wing from tip to tip and the elimination of fuselage interference from the sensitive upper surface. Passenger view was greatly improved, with freedom from wing surface glare. The removal of wing spars from the cabin floor was also helpful in planning flexibility of cabin layout.

The main factor in achieving a high economical speed was undoubtedly the very high aspect ratio wing, designed to achieve as high a proportion of laminar flow as possible. The worst problem in designing such a wing is the achievement of structural integrity with freedom from twisting under aileron movement conditions. The elimination of skin waviness and "quilting" is equally essential. Hagg had previous experience of thin wings of this general type as far back as 1934, when he designed the remarkably successful DH.88 Comet racer which

The design and development team at Fairmile Manor. Left to right: D. G. Riches, assistant experimental manager; C. Chapleo, chief structural engineer; G. P. Jewett, chief development engineer; A. E. Ellison, chief project engineer; J. F. Foss, chief aerodynamicist; H. V. Clarke, chief engineer; A. E. Hagg, technical director and chief designer; F. J. Jupp, experimental manager; J. Johnston, chief draughtsman; G. B. S. Errington, chief test pilot.   *de Havilland Aircraft*

won the MacRobertson Air Race to Australia, and later in the elegant DH.91 Albatross airliner of 1938. Both had wooden skins, half-inch (12.7mm) and one-inch (25.4mm) thickness respectively, with the main stresses being carried by these skins which were capable of taking, and maintaining, a good surface finish. In the A.S.57 90% of the skin stresses were taken by the skin in compression.

The fuselage was an almost perfect streamlined form. This was expensive to build but, as Hagg argued, if the extra cost was spread over five years of operation at a utilisation of 2,000 hours per annum it would be more than covered by the economic advantages of its own level of aerodynamic efficiency and the additional value of speed itself.

The D.H.91 Albatross, a four-engined airliner designed by Arthur Hagg in 1938.
British Airways

Immense care would be necessary in skin rivetting to ensure that the very low drag potential of the design was realised.

The A.S.57 was finalised at an all-up weight of 45,000 lb (18,140 kg), with an 8,000 lb (3,630 kg), 40-passenger payload, later to be increased to 50,000 lb all-up with an 11,000 lb (4,990 kg) 50-passenger payload.

It was considered essential that the new airliner should be capable of accepting a four-propeller-turbine installation, as suitable power plants such as the Rolls-Royce Dart, Armstrong Siddeley Mamba and Napier Naiad were in course of development. Consideration was also being given to a military transport version of the type, the A.S.60, which would fly at an all-up weight of 52,000 lb (23,580 kg).

The Christchurch factory was chosen as the production base, under the control of Major Hereward de Havilland, D.S.O., brother of Sir Geoffrey and joint managing director with J. Liddell. Since 1941 Horsa gliders and Mosquitoes had been built there, and later some Spitfires were converted to Seafires. With the end of the European war production was tailing off as contracts were completed. A 1,700 yard (1,550m) take-off run was available, and there was ample room for expansion of the factory with its already extensive production facilities.

Work commenced immediately on extension of the drawing offices and research laboratories. As soon as this was completed the design team moved from Fairmile Manor to Christchurch. John Jupp, the Portsmouth Experimental Shop manager, was posted to Christchurch to convert the plant and to carry out a world-wide survey of rivetting techniques to establish the best method of meeting the very tight tolerances set down by the Aerodynamics Department.

It was decided after consultation with British European Airways that the all-up weight would ultimately be increased to 52,000 lb (23,580 kg), in line with that of the A.S.60 project. This involved minor alterations to the design of the

The superb streamlining of the Ambassador's engine installation.
Airspeed Limited

undercarriage, some stiffening of the airframe, increased braking power, and the development of automatic pitch coarsening of the propellers to deal with the case of engine failure on take-off without further action by the pilot. Cabin pressurisation produced its own crop of problems in both airframe and engines. De-icing required the development of a thermal system from little-known basic principles, and the electrical system had to be redesigned to provide adequate power for the cyclic heating of propeller blades.

Work commenced on building test specimens, including complete wings and fuselages, a tail unit and a mass of forgings, castings and other components. Many of these were to be tested at Christchurch; others, such as wings and fuselages, were to be sent elsewhere, the wings to Farnborough and the fuselage to Portsmouth Dockyard for pressurisation tests.

By late 1944 the Ministry of Aircraft Production had ordered two prototypes, and a flight deck mock-up was available for comment by potential customers. In 1937 Airspeed had set a new standard of logical cockpit layout in the Oxford trainer, and the A.S.57 followed in this tradition. Many airline pilots were consulted and an outstandingly good layout resulted.

Engine development was a major part of the programme. During the war engine technology had made immense strides and the Bristol Centaurus 18-cylinder sleeve valve radial engine powering the Hawker Tempest II fighter was capable of conversion to the Mark 661 used in the new airliner at a rating of 2,700 h.p.

Cowlings opened for maintenance.
Airspeed Limited

Achieving adequate cooling of this powerful engine without an excessive drag penalty was crucial to success. The final design of the engine nacelles was a remarkable compromise between superb streamlining and high cooling efficiency. The exhausts were designed to pass over the wing and give extra thrust.

Simplicity of maintenance facilities is very important to the airline engineer, as every unnecessary minute the aeroplane spends on the ground is money wasted. A very detailed study of the problem led to the design of a "power egg", with the engine and all its ancillary services in a compact unit which, it was claimed, could be changed in 17 minutes. An electric motor provided power for hydraulic services and the air conditioning plant, so the only ground equipment essential to operation was a portable battery set or "chore-horse" generating set.

By October 1945, early marks of the engine were being flown on type tests in a Vickers Warwick and a fuselage mock-up was available for inspection by potential customers and the press. The new aeroplane had been named Ambassador, a logical progression from the Courier of 1933 and the Envoy of 1934. In 1935 Airspeed had designed a twin-radial-engined high-wing monoplane airliner almost identical with the de Havilland DH.95 Flamingo of 1938, and this had been given the name Ambassador, but it was never built.

The structural and component test programme was accelerating. Many entirely new components manufactured by outside suppliers had to be developed and proved, so close liaison was necessary to ensure that testing and delivery did not fall behind the required time schedule. John Jupp, now works manager, had completed his survey of rivetting techniques. Fourteen months' work produced a system by which a special rivet was punched into an accurately countersunk hole; a special gauge traversed the wing to check every rivet, and a superbly finished wing of the highest aerodynamic efficiency resulted.

The design office was working on variants of the airliner. The A.S.60 Ayrshire military transport with "clamshell" loading doors at the rear of the

An interior view of the Ambassador under construction. *via Aeroplane Monthly*

The fuselage of the prototype Ambassador ready for assembly of wings and engines, May, 1947.
Airspeed Limited

fuselage was shown in model form at Farnborough and at the 1946 S.B.A.C. Show at Radlett. Orders for this machine would have been of immense benefit to the Ambassador programme. During a meeting at Christchurch on 22nd October 1945, a telephone call was received from a very senior Ministry of Aircraft Production official who said that they hoped to place an order for 50 Ayrshires straight from the mock-up stage, but not a single order materialised.

Ministry thinking, and indeed that of British European Airways, was complicated by the existence of two radically new turbo-propeller designs, the Vickers VC 2 Viceroy with four Rolls-Royce Dart engines and the Armstrong Whitworth Apollo with four Armstrong Siddeley Mambas. To further complicate the issue de Havilland was designing the revolutionary DH.106 Comet with pure jet turbines. D.H. realised that if this was successful it would require the use of all their production and technical facilities, so they were certainly lukewarm toward the possibility of orders for the Ayrshire.

In June 1947, the Ambassador prototype was weighed at Christchurch, and it was said that the disposable load would be within 100 lb (45 kg) of the design figure. Prior to its first flight a series of ground hops were made, only minor modifications being required. On 10th July George Errington, with J. Pears as engineer and flight test observer, flew G-AGUA for the first time. The flight lasted 50 minutes, the aircraft behaving well although the centre rudder shed its spring tab and a partial electrical failure caused the loss of some services for a short time.

It was decided that the centre rudder should be fixed and that modifications would be required to the outer rudder tabs to compensate. Resonance tests were carried out whilst this work was in hand, braking equipment for the propellers was fitted and the machine painted in a very attractive livery which enhanced its graceful lines, seldom surpassed in any of the world's aircraft. Perhaps the only slightly discordant note was the angular shape of the fins and rudders which owed more to the need to keep to the maximum overall height than to the dictates of aesthetics.

In September 1947, the Ambassador was demonstrated at the S.B.A.C. Show at Radlett, where the cockpit and controls of the second prototype had been erected as a display feature in the static show. George Errington put on his usual polished demonstration and a very favourable impression was created by this beautiful and quiet aeroplane.

Vickers had received a development contract for their VC.2 on 9th March 1946, and by the time the Ambassador flew it was well advanced, having been

The prototype Ambassador G-AGUA in flight. *Aeroplane Monthly*

re-designated Type 609, later to be Type 630 and named Viscount. By the time the Vickers aircraft flew for the first time on 16th July 1948, the Ambassador had suffered a serious setback, when after 50 hours airborne the bolts retaining the hydraulic actuation ram of the port undercarriage leg failed as the prototype was flying at high speed. The leg dropped and locked in the down position, fortunately without tearing the wing off. All hydraulic fluid was lost through the ruptured piping, making it impossible to lower the flaps for landing, so the Ambassador was landed at fairly high speed on the one locked-down leg. The outcome was a remarkable vindication of the "crashworthiness" of the high wing layout. The wings and engine nacelles were undamaged, and the repairs to the underside of the fuselage were completed within 18 days.

B.E.A., still doubtful about the economics of the turbo-prop Viscount which, in any case, was too small in its original form for their routes, placed a provisional order for 20 Ambassadors in December 1947. This was a totally uneconomic quantity, although it was understood that they were interested in the prop-jet version which could be developed from the second prototype, provision having been made in the design for the installation of gas turbines.

In these days of astronomical development costs, it is interesting to realise that the price quoted for the Ambassador without radio and furnishings was £145,980.

By February 1948, a total of 70 hours of test flying had been completed, and minor alterations to control surfaces and some strengthening of the undercarriage was required before overload tests could be started. The performance was very satisfactory and the single-engine climb-out better than anticipated.

Air Vice-Marshal D. C. T. Bennett, wartime Pathfinder Force commander and director of British South American Airways, inspects the Ambassador prototype with Arthur Hagg.
Aeroplane Monthly

In the meantime Vickers, realising the depth of indecision within B.E.A. over the economics of the turbine-powered Type 609 and its small size, put forward a proposal that a version, the Type 653, with a larger airframe and Centaurus engines should be developed. This was very similar to the Ambassador in size and style but far behind it in time. The Government tried to pressure B.E.A. to order it instead of the untried and unknown Type 609 and George Edwards, the chief designer at Vickers, brought his formidable advocacy to bear upon B.E.A. Vickers pressed on doggedly, ultimately succeeding in producing one of the world's finest airliners, which sold throughout the world in hundreds.

Flight trials soon revealed the Ambassador to have remarkable characteristics in single-engine flying. She was fully controllable with one propeller feathered down to a speed of 110 knots. At the 1948 Farnborough Show George Errington flew the second prototype, G-AKRD, on only one engine from take-off to landing, steering on the ground with the nose wheel. This machine was pressurised and ultimately furnished to airline standards.

British European Airways' hesitation in supporting the new aeroplane was causing considerable concern to Airspeed and, indeed, in Parliament. On 27th July, in the course of a debate on civil aviation, G. S. Lindgren, Parliamentary Secretary to the Ministry of Civil Aviation, stated that the Ambassador was not going into operation until 1952 because B.E.A. did not want it earlier than this. They had spent over £500,000 on developing the Viking, which would be replaced by the Airspeed machine. He went on to say that the Ambassador was just the type which charter people would buy, and, in fact, did buy. "B.E.A. have placed their orders and certain charter operators in this country have now followed their example."

Flight referred to this statement and reported that "In late 1947 Airspeed had warned the Government that unless an immediate decision was made it would soon be necessary to stand off staff. Contrary to the impression conveyed by Mr. Lindgren, B.E.A. had to be talked into placing a large order before any charter company would follow suit, and the firm must have a large initial order if the cost is not to be prohibitive. If the Corporation had shown earlier interest, the prototype could have flown in 1946 and the aircraft be in production now instead of 1952. B.E.A.'s hesitation has probably also lost export orders from continental firms, who may now prefer the Convair 27."

The flight deck of the Ambassador. *Airspeed Limited*

In September 1948, *Flight* published a technical comparison between the Ambassador and the American Convair 27, with considerable advantage to the Ambassador. In the same month, nine months after the announcement of the provisional order for 20 aircraft, the Ministry of Supply confirmed it.

Test flying was proceeding satisfactorily. Arthur Hagg had resigned as chief designer, to be succeeded by George Miles of Miles Aircraft fame. A. E. Ellison, who had joined Hessell Tiltman in the York days, was appointed chief development engineer. On 17th November the Ambassador was flown at 52,000 lb (23,580 kg), at which weight it was ultimately certified. The take-off was made from the 1,300 yard (1,180m) runway at R.A.F. Beaulieu, Hants. Touching down at a weight of 50,000 lb (22,680 kg), the machine stopped in half the length of the runway.

By mid-April 1949, the third aircraft was in the main assembly jigs, the remaining 20 being planned to follow at the rate of two a month. In 18 months of test flying the prototypes accumulated 350 hours. Modifications found necessary were the lightening of the aileron control by altering the contours of the upper surface, oscillation of the tail unit was traced and damped, the undercarriage was moved forward and the wheelbase shortened. Arrangements were also made to permit flexible containers to be fitted inside the integral fuel tanks.

The passenger cabin of the prototype Ambassador.   *Airspeed Limited*

The Ambassador fuselage en route to Portsmouth Dockyard for pressure tests.

Airspeed Limited

In June the national press made a sensational story of the failure of the wing in the structural test rig at Farnborough. They did not, of course, point out that a sound method of designing a wing is to do so to exactly the specified strength factor. If tests then prove the structure to be inadequate, appropriate stiffening can be built in. Hitherto we had tended to build wings well over strength, and the penalty was unnecessary weight. Nevertheless, it was a serious setback to the programme and much midnight oil was burned to rectify the wing. On 6th December the wing passed the target of 100% design strength figure at Farnborough, the data being recorded on a Polygraph Electronic Strain Recorder designed by Airspeed. Ultimate failure occurred at 120% design load, and the structure weight had been increased by a mere 280lb (126 kg) for a strength gain of 40%.

The fuselage was tested by submerging it in a basin at Portsmouth Dockyard, filling it with water and pressuring it to failure point. The maximum requirements were easily exceeded. The failure produced the surprising phenomenon that the structure collapsed inwards.

In January 1950, George Errington, demonstrating a simulated engine failure on take-off at Hurn Airport, failed to realise that he was approaching a rising section of the runway and landed back on it with his undercarriage retracted. Temporary repairs were carried out and the Ambassador flown back to Christchurch. Once again the "crash-worthiness" of the type had been proved, but it was a demonstration which Airspeed could have done without.

The production prototype G-ALFR also came to grief at Hurn in July, not long after its first flight in May, when the starboard leg partially retracted during the landing run. Damage was only slight, the aircraft being flown back to Christchurch three days later. The accident was caused by a fracture in the torque link which allowed the leg to oscillate directionally, causing failure of the down-lock mechanism.

Further trouble was in store for this aircraft on 13th November when an extraordinary accident occurred as the indirect result of pressure being applied to a seriously delayed test programme, in the course of which B.E.A. had asked Airspeed to try to extend the C.G. limit further forward to reduce constraints on passenger cabin loading. At the time it appeared disastrous, but surprisingly little damage was done to the airframe.

On the day in question the Air Registration Board test pilot was due to have assessed the handling of the Ambassador at the new C. G. forward limits. The establishment of these limits was the task given to test pilot Ron Clear. The test schedule required satisfactory handling to be demonstrated during landings made from a stabilised approach condition from a height of 1,000 feet (305m) in the full flap-down, power-off configuration. In order that the characteristics could be quantified a desynn indicator was fitted in the cockpit, enabling the pilot to see the position of the elevator in relation to the total elevator movement available.

Ron Clear carried out a number of circuits, during each of which the aircraft was stalled and the elevator angle and stick force recorded before the approach and landing. The ballast was moved forward in small increments for each test. A condition was finally reached in which the loading was such that although the stick force was approaching the maximum desired (50 lb, 22.68 kg), the elevator

Ambassador G-ALFR after the mishap at Hurn airport in July, 1950.   *Airspeed Limited*

desynn confirmed that some 4 degrees of elevator movement remained available at the stall.

The approach was made in the scheduled configuration and the landing flare commenced at about 50 feet (15m); to his dismay Ron then realised that he had already applied the maximum available elevator but the radius of flare was too great for a satisfactory landing. He immediately applied full throttle. True to form, the Centaurus engines coughed before bellowing forth at full power just as the nose wheel struck the ground, the few seconds delay in the engines giving full power depriving the elevators of much needed slipstream effect at the crucial moment.

The heavy impact of the nosewheel and resultant recoil of the fully compressed oleo shock absorber leg caused the nose of the aircraft to rotate violently just as the main wheels struck the ground. The machine's undamped accelerometer recorded an impact acceleration of 14 g, two and a half times the maximum designed value. The result of this excessive loading was that the engines parted company with the nacelles and just went straight ahead. In Ron Clear's memorable words "The glider climbed over them to a height of some 40 feet (12m) with the control column now on the forward stop and the C.G. well aft of the aft limit." A safe landing was eventually made before he reached the edge of the airfield, with all the tyres flat and the aircraft some four tons lighter.

One of the flight observers who was about to terminate flying duties due to a severe back complaint was sitting in the navigator's seat when he felt the fearsome impact of the "landing". Being, no doubt, convinced that his career was about to terminate in a holocaust, he was the first to evacuate by the forward cabin door, but was possibly unaware that due to the fully extended main undercarriage oleos and the tail-down attitude of the aircraft the floor height had increased to about 10 feet (3m).

Clear, having brought the "glider" safely to rest and being aware of the possible fire hazard from ruptured fuel lines, lost no time in following his crew in vacating the ship. As he ruefully examined the engineless bulkheads, clear of all accessories and fittings, and saw the engines with their propellers wrapped around them like grotesque petals, the thought crossed his mind that this unusual exercise was indeed going to take some explaining. His reverie was suddenly interrupted by the excited voice of his observer announcing "It's all right!"

"It's alright?" said Ron tightly. "I can see nothing alright about it!"

"My back!" said the man. "It's all right now, my fall must have put it right!" The pilot was neither terribly interested nor sympathetic at that moment.

Clear's skill in handling such a potentially catastrophic situation avoided major damage to the aircraft, which was flying again three weeks later. The

Above: "Finished with engines" — the Ambassador after the accident at Christchurch on 13th November, 1950.

Right: The scene from the air, with G-ALFR lying at the end of the skid-marks.

Below: The engines.
All Airspeed Limited

investigation proved that a series of related minor factors was responsible for the incident. The last four degrees of elevator movement, which should have given a very adequate margin to initiate the flare-out, was totally ineffective as, at that angle, the elevators were stalled. Since the air speed indicator was independent, with no balance pipe fitted, there was a slight position error compounded by a gusty cross wind blowing 60 degrees off the centre line of the landing path, causing the captain's A.S.I. to over-read with the result that the true air speed was lower than intended.

This unfortunate setback terminated in a felicitous touch when, at a works dinner several weeks later, George Errington congratulated Ron Clear on his masterly handling of the affair and presented him with a small model of a ship's engine room telegraph. The handle was set at ''FINISHED WITH ENGINES.''

Nevertheless, these various problems caused still further delay to a programme already running late due to continuing indecision at ministerial and B.E.A. level. Christchurch were well advanced with G-AMAD, the first production aircraft, and the flagship G-ALZN, named *Elizabethan*, was almost finished. B.E.A. adopted Elizabethan as the class name.

On 24th November *Flight* commented ''Australian National Airlines and Trans-Australia Airlines are both keen on the Ambassador, and New Zealand and India are potential customers. Aer Lingus Irish Airlines are looking for fleet replacements. Spain and Portugal are potential customers whilst Turkey and Greece have 50 DC.3 Dakotas in service. S.A.S. Scandinavian Airlines have 30 DC.3s which require replacement. K.L.M., Sabena and Swissair have opted for the Convair Metropolitan. So,'' *Flight* concluded, ''the whole of the sterling area is open to the Ambassador.''

G-AMAD, *Sir Francis Drake*, first flew on 12th January 1951. It was scheduled for delivery to B.E.A. on 15th January, with a further five aircraft by 15th March 1951, but it was obviously impossible to meet this timetable. In May, with an Airspeed and airline flight crew, the aircraft flew for 52½ hours in four days. The Air Registration Board required 250 hours' flying before a Certificate of Airworthiness could be issued. By 20th May 160 hours had been flown.

In April George Errington carried out tests on the long runway built for the Brabazon airliner at Filton to check the ability of the machine to take off safely at full weight on one engine. At 52,000 lb (25,580 kg) control was perfect from initial roll to a maximum height of 15,000 feet (4,570 m). *Flight* commented ''These are possibly the heaviest loads ever taken off and flown to such heights on the power of a single engine.''

On 21st July 1951, the final merger between Airspeed and de Havilland was announced, all the Airspeed shares now being in the possession of the company which had taught the two founders of Airspeed, Hessell Tiltman and Nevil Shute Norway, their trade in the 'Twenties. In future the firm was to be known as the Airspeed Division of the de Havilland Aircraft Company Limited. It was already involved in DH. work, having been entrusted in 1950 with the development of a twin-seat trainer version of the Vampire fighter; the outcome, the Vampire T Mk II, found favour with the air forces of a number of countries.

By the beginning of August G-AMAD, G-ALZN and G-ALZP plus the two development prototypes G-AGUA and G-AKRD had flown 1,550 hours. A Centaurus 661 engine had completed 500 hours' running in the DH. tunnel at Hatfield and a similar engine had flown 200 hours in G-AMAD. On 19th July the Air Registration Board issued a normal Certificate of Airworthiness for the A.S.57 Ambassador.

The flagship, G-ALZN, was formally handed over to B.E.A. at London Airport on 21st August. George Errington flew it from Christchurch to Heathrow, where the aircraft and its documents were handed over to Capt. C. E. F. Riley, the airline's Chief Pilot, who taxied it away to its new hangar.

The Ambassador operated the London to Paris service on 3rd September. The seating layout was unusual, with front and rearward facing seats. There was a tendency for rearward facing passengers to slide off the seats during the climb and particularly on take-off, but vibration was minimal, the traditional glass of water on the table remaining undisturbed. The joke at B.E.A. conversion courses was that when an engine cut without warning the Captain took several minutes to decide which one was out; so much for its reputation as a very docile aeroplane.

Flight said "Now that the Ambassador is in service other operator interest should increase. This highly competitive aircraft looks like being one of the

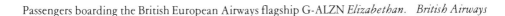

Passengers boarding the British European Airways flagship G-ALZN *Elizabethan*. *British Airways*

The British European Airways flagship in flight.   *British Airways*

biggest money earners in the airline industry, and should be earning its keep ten years from now.''

Development problems delayed delivery of the other aircraft, the power plants produced excessive drag and performance was not up to the airline specification, engine temperature also being too low. Tropical trials were carried out at Khartoum in August and September, when the production prototype G-ALFR was flown out by a team led by R. E. Clear. He was uneasy at the maximum loading, predicted by the aerodynamicist in the crew, at which the machine would take off on one engine at an ambient temperature of 35 degrees centigrade (95 degrees fahrenheit). After discussion with his flight test observer he accepted the challenge and, at an all-up weight of 49,000 lb (22,226 kg), cut the starboard engine on take-off at 105 knots. It was impossible to climb and too late to abort. He retracted the undercarriage near the end of the runway at an airspeed which had hardly increased by a knot, thinking that damage would be minimised if they subsided upon the scrubland beyond the perimeter. The aircraft did not sink, thanks to ground effect, and to his relief speed slowly increased over the flat terrain and he was able to climb just high enough to circle for a landing. There were problems with oil cooling at these elevated temperatures, but handling techniques to overcome them were established. The flights to and from Khartoum were a good augury for the reliability and performance of the Ambassador in service.

At the end of October de Havilland issued a statement explaining the delays in delivering the aircraft and saying that B.E.A. had requested certain modifications to bring the production machines up to the specification negotiated in 1948. The main problems were:

1. Conditioned cabin air too hot for summer operations, and there was insufficient circulation of air. De-odorising and filter units and also a cold air unit were to be installed.
2. Radio equipment performance was not adequate in poor weather flying through busy control zones. A modified unit was ready for test.
3. Cruising performance was 7½% down on specification due to cooling drag losses being greater than the original estimate. Work was proceeding on modifications to the cowlings.

The end of 1951 saw the resignation of George Miles as chief designer and the appointment of W. A. Tamblin, a senior de Havilland designer, to take charge of design and development at Christchurch under the overall direction of R. E. Bishop at Hatfield.

By this time, however, the writing was on the wall for the Ambassador. Vickers had developed their turbo-prop Viscount design to a point where, on 28th August 1950, the prototype Model 700 had made its first flight. In September of that year it created a tremendous impression at the Farnborough Show by flying past on one engine, and an outer one at that. B.E.A. and the foreign airlines who had shown interest in the Ambassador realised immediately that the Viscount was the airliner of the future. In July the prototype of the smaller Model 630, of which 20 were on order for B.E.A., had made history with the first fare-paying passengers travelling by turbo-prop airliner from Northolt to Paris. The passengers were deeply impressed.

Various proving flights were made with the Ambassador and, on 13th March 1952, the first scheduled flight was made on the London to Paris service. By the end of March six aircraft were in service for training or scheduled flights. In the first three weeks of operation a million passenger miles was achieved with 3,430 passengers. Problems were minimal and crews and passengers were delighted with this beautiful and comfortable aeroplane, easy to fly and very stable, giving a comfortable ride with a good view through the large windows.

Captain R. E. Gillman, D.F.C., D.F.M. one of the senior Elizabethan captains, said ''The days of bumbling through the weather below 10,000 feet are over, airline flying, from the pilot's point of view is becoming a civilised affair, and our knees do not get wet when it rains.''

Flight had by this time revised its optimistic view of the prospects for the Ambassador. H. A. Taylor wrote on 9th May ''. . . Time, in terms of technical setbacks in relation to the target dates, defeated it. Had the Ambassador become B.E.A.'s working Elizabethan in the spring of 1951 its chances in the overseas market should have been good . . . By the time the still limping paces were being shown in autumn 1951 the operators were losing interest and production capacity at Christchurch was engulfed in military and other work. No doubt some capacity will still remain after the last of B.E.A.'s aircraft come off the line and almost anything can be done by an organisation as big and experienced as D.H. Enterprises if a demand for the aircraft appears. But the fact is . . . we have, in this country, probably passed the point of no return in the transition from pistons to turbines . . . And DH.s were probably right in preferring to concentrate on the more important business of Comet IIs, IIIs and IVs to meet American competition in the fifties.''

On 16th June the famous London to Paris midday luxury Silver Wing service was reintroduced. First flown by the three-engined Armstrong Whitworth Argosy in 1926, this all-first-class service set very high standards of cuisine, with champagne freely available. The timetable was rescheduled to give an extra ten minutes to complete service of the meal.

In July 1952, it was reported that in the first three months of scheduled flying an average of seven Elizabethans flew 1,640 revenue hours with 20,100 passengers over 301,000 aircraft miles. The ninth aircraft, with a refrigeration unit in the starboard nacelle, had been delivered. Hope was expressed that work in hand on the cooling drag problem would produce an extra 10 m.p.h. (16 km/hr) in cruising speed. Following the strip of the first pair of Centaurus 661

The interior of an Elizabethan on the Silver Wing service to Paris.   *British Airways*

engines the A.R.B. agreed to the increase in overhaul time from 250 hours to 500 hours.

The B.E.A. report for 1952/53 stated that the 12 Elizabethans in service flew 2,117,000 revenue miles, carrying 122,400 passengers and 1,240 tons of freight and mail. They earned £1,781,600 at a load factor of 64.4% and made a profit of £322,400. The report concluded "In view of the economically difficult routes on which the Elizabethan is operating and the early difficulties encountered, this result is not unsatisfactory." Almost a case of damning with faint praise.

The report for 1953/54 showed a distinct thawing of attitude to the Elizabethan, stating that the fleet of 20 aircraft was in its second year of operation and "These fine aeroplanes have now settled down and are operating to high standards of serviceability and regularity. Their wide and comfortable cabins beneath the high wing are very popular with the travelling public."

The opposition also received high praise, the "outstanding event of the year" being "the introduction into regular airline services of the world's first prop-turbine transport aircraft". The Viscount had amassed 15,400 hours of revenue flying carrying 146,454 passengers to show a net profit of £301,000 out of earnings of £3,150,000.

In the 1954/55 report it was declared that "Much of B.E.A.'s success (in increasing its traffic share) must be credited to the Elizabethans and Viscounts which, for the first complete year, operated almost all B.E.A.'s International Services". The Elizabethan flew 6,418,220 aircraft miles in 37,685 hours producing 32,209,780 capacity ton miles, being 33.8% of the B.E.A. total output.

By February 1955, the significant figure of one million passengers was reached and utilisation had reached 2,009 hours per annum. At the peak of the summer traffic each aircraft flew 6¼ hours per day, as the report commented, "An excellent performance for a fleet operating over an average sector distance of only 299 statute miles (480 km)." In July 1954, profitability had been increased still further by an increase in all-up weight by 2,500 lb (1,132 kg) to 55,000 lb (24,915 kg). The report continued "Now in its fourth year of operation with B.E.A., the Elizabethan is very popular with passengers who admire its elegant lines and spacious cabins . . . The Elizabethan has assumed, easily and naturally, that air of quiet luxury associated since before the war with the de-luxe Silver Wing service to Paris."

In spite of these encouraging comments and the splendid safety record of the aircraft, there were still problems. Captain Gillman was flying "Zulu Uniform" to London at cruising altitude, with the outside air temperature minus 20 degrees centigrade, when suddenly the elevator control seized solid. He was forced to consider a landing using only power settings to achieve changes of trim, so spent some time experimenting to find out the effect of varying power

on trim. His findings did nothing to encourage him to think that the landing would be other than a very hairy affair. He began a long flat approach, and at the final stage he was relieved to find that he had full control again. A safe landing was made.

The aircraft was almost dismantled in an attempt to discover the cause. Nothing was found until a very sharp-eyed inspector noticed discoloration on the outside edge of the air-conditioning vent where it passed through the rear pressure bulkhead, very close to the elevator control cables. Passengers' breath passing out through the vent had condensed on the cold metal, and the ice build-up had grown until it embraced the cables, locking them solidly. Altitude test flying had never revealed such a situation since no passengers had been carried.

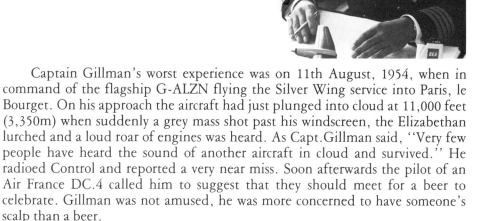

Captain R. E. Gillman,
D.F.C., D.F.M.,
M.R.Ae.S., M.R.I.N.
British Airways

Captain Gillman's worst experience was on 11th August, 1954, when in command of the flagship G-ALZN flying the Silver Wing service into Paris, le Bourget. On his approach the aircraft had just plunged into cloud at 11,000 feet (3,350m) when suddenly a grey mass shot past his windscreen, the Elizabethan lurched and a loud roar of engines was heard. As Capt.Gillman said, "Very few people have heard the sound of another aircraft in cloud and survived." He radioed Control and reported a very near miss. Soon afterwards the pilot of an Air France DC.4 called him to suggest that they should meet for a beer to celebrate. Gillman was not amused, he was more concerned to have someone's scalp than a beer.

Inspection on the ground revealed that the two aircraft had, in fact, collided. The starboard outer propeller of the DC.4 had almost torn the wing tip off the Elizabethan, only the fact that one of the aircraft was slightly banked averting a hideous disaster. French air traffic control was found to be responsible for the incident.

An Elizabethan on a proving flight
t Nice, 5th March, 1952.
British Airways

Generally the safety record of the Elizabethan was extremely good. Two aircraft shed nose wheels in the air and, by an odd coincidence, the pilot in each case was Captain Jack Cooke, who received the Queen's Commendation for Valuable Services in the Air for his skilful landing of the first of these aircraft.

By the time B.E.A. issued their report for 1955/56 Viscounts were replacing the Elizabethan, 36 of the prop-turbine airliners and 19 Elizabethans being in service. G-AMAB *Sir Francis Bacon* had been written off in an emergency landing at Dusseldorf after one of the propellers had gone into reverse pitch and the drag had proved so high that it was impossible to remain airborne. There were no fatalities. Thereafter the pitch reversing mechanism was disconnected on all Elizabethans.

The next year's report revealed that 55 Viscounts were in service and only 13 Elizabethans, the report stating that the type was due for complete replacement in 1958.

The worst disaster in which an Elizabethan was involved occurred on 6th February 1958. G-ALZU *Lord Burghley* had been chartered to take the Manchester United football team to Belgrade. After a refuelling stop at Munich on the return flight Captain James Thain attempted a take-off in conditions of snow and ice. He aborted the first attempt as he observed variations in the boost pressure on one engine. He tried again, once more the pressure fluctuated so he returned to the terminal.

Fifteen minutes later Thain taxied out again to the runway. Given the green from the control tower, he opened the throttles to take-off power and accelerated down the runway, the aircraft reaching 117 knots with a slightly surging port engine. Then to Thain's dismay speed dropped to 105 knots and the aircraft showed no tendency to lift off. It crashed through the perimeter fence and hit a house, tearing the port wing off and slewing the machine round, whereupon it caught fire. Of the 44 people aboard 23 died, among them the co-pilot, eight British football stars and eight leading sports writers.

A German official at the scene of the crash told a public enquiry in Munich that the crash was caused by the failure of the pilot to remove snow and ice from the wings. This could not possibly explain the deceleration which Thain experienced from 117 knots to 105 knots, yet the captain was found to be responsible. He lost his licence and his job.

Thain, convinced that the real explanation was slush on the runway, carried out private experiments to prove his contention and found evidence elsewhere of similar occurrences. He could not obtain a hearing, however, as the British Government was reluctant to cast doubt on the findings of a foreign power.

Justice was finally done as the result of a chance remark made by Prime Minister Harold Wilson at a dinner of the Manchester United Football Club. He said that he thought that Thain had been badly treated. The Press picked up the remark and gave it wide publicity, resulting in the holding of a further inquiry in London at which the German conclusions were reversed and Capt. Thain exonerated from blame. It was too late. Financially ruined and exhausted by his years of struggle for vindication, he died soon afterwards.

The last service flown under B.E.A. colours by an Elizabethan was from Cologne to London on 30th July 1958. During their period of service the fleet carried 2,500,000 passengers on 90,000 flights totalling one thousand million passenger miles at an average load factor of 67.5%. So the Ambassador, to revert to its type name, ended its short career with B.E.A., overtaken by the brilliantly successful Viscount.

Captain Ron Gillman, who had been loaned by B.E.A. to Napiers to evaluate the Napier Eland-powered conversion of G-ALFR, is convinced that if the turbine-powered version had been developed it would have been even more successful than the Viscount. This machine was demonstrated at the Farnborough Show in 1955. B.E.A., having lost interest in all versions of the Ambassador, in 1961 converted this one back to standard with Centaurus engines and sold it to Dan-Air for charter services.

In February 1959, Captain Gillman was posted to Rolls Royce to take part in the development programme of the Tyne propeller turbine to be fitted to the new Vanguard aircraft in production for B.E.A. With twice the power for which it was designed, the Ambassador/Tyne test bed was described by Captain Gillman as "a very hot ship indeed". In his book *Croydon to Concorde* he describes how the aircraft could be climbed at over 4,000 feet per minute

An Elizabethan at Frankfurt, West Germany. *British Airways*

(1,220 m/min), a rate comparable to the current military fighter, but it was too late. The Viscount was too well entrenched and de Havillands had put into the Portsmouth and Christchurch factories assemblies for the Comet and Sea Vixen aircraft.

In August 1961, it was announced in the *Portsmouth Evening News* that in the next 12 months approximately 1,500 workers, three quarters of the labour force, would be declared redundant. In October, 1962, the last completed de Havilland assembly left the factory, leaving only the small No. 2 Factory employing 500 people. By the end of the decade this, too, and the great factory at Christchurch, had closed down.

All that was left of Airspeed Limited was a rather scruffy little road on the industrial estate which had developed around the aerodrome called Norway Road, after the co-founder of the company, Nevil Shute Norway. Hessell Tiltman, Sir Alan Cobham, Lord Grimthorpe and all the other creators of the Airspeed tradition were only commemorated in the memories of the men who worked for them and built the Airspeed tradition.

The author was, coincidentally, at the Portsmouth factory on the day it closed. George Statham, the works manager, said, "I came here as a de Havilland man but I soon recognised the strength of the Airspeed tradition. Frankly, I look upon myself as an Airspeed man now." For a D.H. man to say such a thing is a remarkable tribute to Airspeed.

Opposite page: The Rolls Royce Tyne-powered Elizabethan.

Captain R. E. Gillman, D.F.C., D.F.M.

Below: The second prototype Ambassador G-AKRD fitted with an icing spray bar attachment to simulate ice ingestion while being used as a test bed for the Bristol Proteus turbo-prop engine.

Captain R. E. Gillman, D.F.C., D.F.M.

The Ambassadors continued to fly the flag mainly under charter company colours, although Shell Petroleum and Decca also operated two of them. The King of Jordan bought two, one as a troop carrier, ultimately re-sold to Dan-Air for conversion back to passenger use.

Mr Frank Horridge, managing director of Dan-Air, told the author that their utilisation of the Ambassador was higher than that of any other operator and, by using dispersant oils which overcame problems inherent in sleeve valve engines, they were able to increase periods between overhaul to 3,000 hours. He thought the Centaurus was the finest piston engine ever installed in an airliner, and that the Ambassador was an outstanding airliner which should have been developed. He agreed with Captain Ron Gillman that if it had been fitted with prop-turbines it would have been superior to the Viscount.

So Airspeed's last and finest aeroplane followed the path of most of the earlier designs, fine aircraft, insufficiently capitalised, insufficiently developed and insufficiently promoted in the market. The survivors finished their careers as they began, as safe comfortable aircraft making good profits for their operators.

Two met with disaster, G-ALZX in Dan-Air service being damaged beyond repair in an overrun accident at Beauvais in 1966 and the first production aircraft G-AMAD, converted to freight work by B.K.S., being destroyed in a crash when landing at Heathrow on 3rd July 1968. It was landing with a cargo of eight horses, five grooms and a crew of three when it suddenly began to bank to the left until the port wing tip and undercarriage touched the ground, slewing the aircraft through 30 degrees. The machine took the tail off a Trident parked outside the uncompleted No. 1 Terminal, into which it then crashed, killing four people and injuring 31 others in the aircraft and on the ground.

Dan-Air's Ambassador G-ALZO.   *Aeroplane Monthly*

Above: Autair's
Ambassador G-ALZZ.
Aeroplane Monthly

Right: Flying in style,
1952. Boarding the
Silver Wing service to
Paris.   *British Airways*

Elizabethans of British European Airways outside the hangars at London Airport.   *British Airways*

The Napier Eland-powered Elizabethan G-ALFR.

The accident was found to have resulted from the failure of the port flap actuation rod, which caused this flap to retract and the starboard one to lower a further 10 degrees to 50 degrees, a circumstance which it was quite beyond the capacity of the pilot to rectify.

Today only one Ambassador remains at Lasham Airfield where Dan-Air preserve it as a museum piece. Long may its beautiful lines gladden the senses, and may it soon be preserved under cover.

Autair's Ambassador G-ALZZ on lease to Skyways.   *via Aeroplane Monthly*

Airspeed Projects

A S with most aircraft companies, Airspeed designed many aircraft which did not reach even the prototype stage.

The A.S.15 heavy bomber of 1935 was a remarkable project, very advanced for its time. Like a huge four-engined Wellington, 166 feet (50.6m) in span, it was heavily armed with twin turrets in the nose. A top speed of 215 m.p.h. (346 km/hr) was envisaged. The Air Ministry considered that such a major undertaking was beyond Airspeed's capability.

An odd concept was the A.S.27, originally designed as a slow-flying coastal patrol aircraft. When Professor Lindemann, later Lord Cherwell, Winston Churchill's scientific adviser, was investigating defence against bombers he had the idea of using a squadron of these aircraft trailing wires with bombs on the end to entangle the enemy aircraft. Mercifully it was not developed.

In February 1936, Tiltman submitted to the Air Ministry, at their invitation, a 113-page brochure and specification of a bomber, A.S.29 to Spec B1/35. It was a most advanced all-metal aircraft very similar to the Boeing B.17 Flying Fortress. The brochure was totally ignored by the Ministry, and Airspeed did not even receive an acknowledgement of its receipt.

At the end of 1935 an invitation to tender for a high-speed fighter was received. Since 1933 Norway had brooded upon a quite revolutionary concept of an aircraft with the pilot far aft, and if possible above the main airframe so that he could judge his landings extremely accurately. His discussions with Tiltman led to the A.S.31 with a Rolls-Royce Kestrel engine and the pilot in a nacelle at the tail. A wind tunnel model gave exceptional test results, but no support was forthcoming from the Ministry.

A.S.32-35 was a series of handsome transport aircraft, designed for in-flight refuelling.

A.S.37 was a rather striking flying boat target machine, superseded by the Queen Wasp design.

A.S.47 was a twin tandem-engined fighter with Napier Sabre engines, whilst the A.S.56 was an extremely elegant Sabre-engined wooden fighter with a low drag annular radiator. This, and the A.S.49 trainer, reached the mock-up stage at Hatfield in 1940, with a good chance that orders would be placed. On 3rd October 1940, a marauding Junkers 88 bombed the de Havilland works, both mock-ups and all the drawings being destroyed.

Tiltman, as technical director, had other crosses to bear. For example, the very senior Airspeed director who suggested that a rudimentary fighter should be built with a bomb mounted on a long probe at the nose. It was intended that

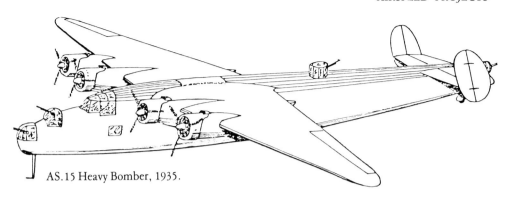

AS.15 Heavy Bomber, 1935.

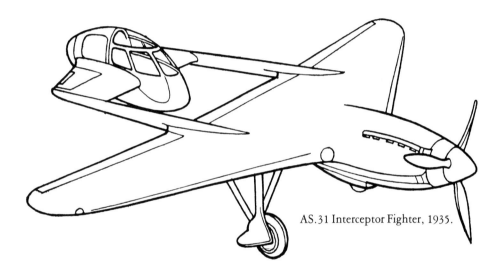

AS.31 Interceptor Fighter, 1935.

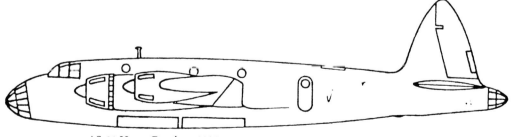

AS.29 Heavy Bomber, 1935.

the fighter should ram the enemy bomber, leaving the bomb inside it with a time fuse. Tiltman, almost speechless, tactfully commented that he considered that if this idea was commonplace the invention of the machine gun would be hailed as a great step forward.

A detailed study of the Airspeed projects reveals the very advanced thinking in the design office of this small company. But for the prejudice which existed, originally, in the Society of British Aircraft Constructors and the Air Ministry and, probably, within de Havillands in the later stages, to say nothing of the chronic shortage of finance that handicapped them throughout their existence, there is little doubt that they would have been among the leaders. They certainly had the technical ability.

It can probably be argued that without the de Havilland finance they would not have survived the ending of wartime contracts. It was unfortunate that they did not have access to independent capital and were forced into a quasi-competitive situation with their own parent company. If that parent had been a powerful organisation, not involved in building airliners, the Ambassador could have emerged as the great British success in world airline service, as Captain Gillman of B.E.A. and Mr Horridge of Dan-Air were both convinced it would have been if turbine powered.

The 'Sixties saw a drastic change in aviation funding. No longer were any individual British companies able to provide capital for major aircraft designs. Collaboration or merger, nationally or internationally, was the only way to survival. Handley-Page, one of the greatest of them, refused merger proposals and did not survive. Airspeed went the way of de Havilland, Bristols, Shorts, Vickers and the rest, into the monolithic British Aerospace.

So all the great names have gone.

AIRSPEED TYPE DESIGNATIONS

Type No.	Name and Identifying Characteristics	Year of First Flight	Type No.	Name and Identifying Characteristics	Year of First Flight
AS-1	Tern. High-performance sailplane	1931	AS-5C	Experimental Courier (Napier Rapier)	1934
AS-2	Glider project.		AS-5J	Courier (Armstrong Siddeley Cheetah IX)	1935
AS-3	Two-seater biplane project.		AS-6	Envoy. Series I. Six/eight-passenger, twin-engined monoplane with retractable under-carriage (two Wolseley A.R.9)	1934
AS-4	Ferry. Ten-passenger, three-engined biplane (one D.H. Gipsy III and two D.H. Gipsy II)	1932			
AS-5	Courier. Five/six-seater monoplane with retractable undercarriage	1933	AS-6A	Envoy. Series I (two Armstrong Siddeley Lynx IVc)	1934
AS-5A	Courier I (Armstrong Siddeley Lynx IVc)	1933	AS-6B	Envoy. Series I. Seaplane project (two Wolseley A.R.9.)	
AS-5B	Courier II (Armstrong Siddeley Cheetah V)	1933			

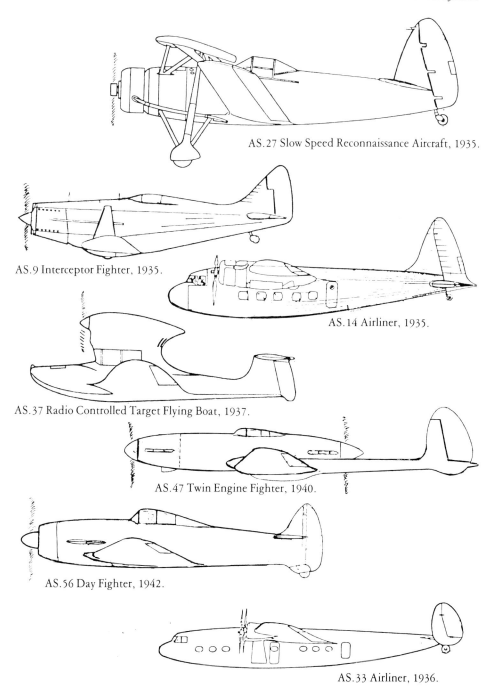

AS.27 Slow Speed Reconnaissance Aircraft, 1935.

AS.9 Interceptor Fighter, 1935.

AS.14 Airliner, 1935.

AS.37 Radio Controlled Target Flying Boat, 1937.

AS.47 Twin Engine Fighter, 1940.

AS.56 Day Fighter, 1942.

AS.33 Airliner, 1936.

Type No.	Name and Identifying Characteristics	Year of First Flight
AS-6C	Envoy. Series I. Seaplane project (two Armstrong Siddeley Lynx IVc.)	
AS-6	Envoy. Series II. Fitted with flaps and increased tailplane area. Suffix "D" denotes two Wright Whirlwind; suffix "E" denotes two Walter Castor II; suffix "F" denotes photographic survey project; suffix "G" denotes two Wolseley Scorpio I	1935
AS-6	Envoy. Series III. Fitted with flaps, ply-covered wing and tailplane with further increased area. Suffix "E" denotes two Walter Castor II; suffix "H" denotes two Wolseley Aries III; suffix "J" denotes two Armstrong Siddeley Cheetah IX; suffix "K" denotes two Wolseley Scorpio II	1936
AS-6Jm	Envoy. Series III. Convertible for military use (two Armstrong Siddeley Cheetah IX)	1936
AS-6Jc	Envoy. Series III. Civil version of 6Jm	1936
AS-7	Military. Envoy project.	
AS-7J	Military Envoy project (two Armstrong Siddeley Cheetah VI.)	
AS-7K	Military Envoy project (two Wolseley Scorpio II).	
AS-8	Viceroy. Special long-range racing version of Envoy (two Armstrong Siddeley Cheetah VI)	1934
AS-9	Interceptor fighter project. Eight-gun, low-wing, strut-braced monoplane. (Napier Dagger, or engine of similar power.)	
AS-10	Oxford I. General-purpose advanced trainer to specification T.23/36 (two Armstrong Siddeley Cheetah X)	1937
AS-10	Oxford II. Crew-training version (two Armstrong Siddeley Cheetah X)	1938
AS-10	Oxford Ambulance (two Armstrong Siddeley Cheetah X)	1938
AS-10	Oxford II. Experimental machine with twin fins and rudders for spinning tests (two Armstrong Siddeley Cheetah X)	1939
AS-10	Oxford II. Experimental aircraft with Rotol constant-speed propellers (two Armstrong Siddeley Cheetah XV)	1939
AS-10	Oxford II. Experimental MacLaren undercarriage (two Armstrong Siddeley Cheetah X)	1939
AS-10	Oxford II. Experimental aircraft (two D.H. Gipsy Queen IV)	1940
AS-10	Oxford III. Project. Fitted with Armstrong Cheetah XV engines, constant-speed propellers and additional equipment.	
AS-10	Oxford IV. Projected crew-training version of Oxford III.	
AS-11	Courier. Projected all-metal version for Canadian market.	
AS-12	Four-engine aircraft project.	
AS-13	Type number not used.	
AS-14	Ambassador. Twin-engine, sixteen-passenger, high-wing transport project. (Two Bristol Pegasus.)	
AS-15	Projected day and night bomber.	
AS-15A	Projected passenger version of AS-15.	
AS-16	Fokker F.22. Four-engine, high-wing transport.	
AS-17	Fokker D.17. Single-seat fighter (Rolls-Royce Kestrel).	
AS-18	Variant of AS-17.	
AS-19	Fokker D.19. Single-seat fighter (Rolls-Royce Kestrel).	
AS-20	Fokker F.36. Four-engine, high-wing transport.	
AS-21	Fokker D.20. Single-seat fighter.	
AS-22	Fokker C.10. Two-seater fighter.	
AS-22A	Fokker C.10. Floatplane.	
AS-23	Douglas DC-2.	
AS-24	Long-range mail-carrying version of AS-14.	
AS-25	Number not allocated.	
AS-26	Car-carrying biplane project.	
AS-27	Special defence aircraft project. Irving-wing biplane and high-wing monoplane versions.	
AS-28	Twin-engine passenger transport project.	
AS-29	Bomber to specification B.1/35 (four Bristol Aquila, or four Rolls-Royce Goshawk).	
AS-30	Queen Wasp. Radio-controlled gunnery target to specification Q.32/35 (Armstrong Siddeley Cheetah IX)	1937

Type No.	Name and Identifying Characteristics	Year of First Flight
AS-31	Projected fighter, to specification F.35/35. Two booms, cockpit in tail, eight guns.	
AS-32	Projected airliner. (Four Bristol Aquila or Libra.)	
AS-33	Projected twenty-four-seater airliner. (Four Bristol Aquila or Libra.)	
AS-34	Projected twelve to fifteen-seater airliner. (Four Armstrong Siddeley Cheetah X.)	
AS-34A	Projected twelve to fifteen-seater airliner. (Four Wolseley Scorpio II engines.)	
AS-35	Projected twelve to fifteen-seater airliner. (Four de Havilland Gipsy Six.)	
AS-36	Two-seater trainer project to specification T.1/37.	
AS-37	Radio-controlled target flying-boat project to specification Q.8/37. (D.H. Gipsy Six Series II.)	
AS-38	Communications aircraft project. Modification of AS-30 Queen Wasp.	
AS-39	Fleet Shadower. Carrier-borne observation aircraft built to specification S.23/37. (Four Pobjoy Niagara V)	1940
AS-40	Oxford civil conversion for radio research	1938
AS-41	Experimental Oxford. (Two Alvis Leonides)	1946
AS-42	Oxford I for New Zealand to specification T.39/37	1938
AS-43	Survey version of AS-42	1938
AS-44	Projected Oxford replacement.	
AS-45	Single-engine trainer to specification T.4/39. (Bristol Mercury VIII)	1941
AS-46	Oxford V: Series I. Canadian "winterised" version of Oxford with two Pratt & Whitney Wasp Juniors, and Hamilton c.s. airscrews. Oxford V: Series II. Similar to Series I, but with no cabin heating or provision for oil warming	1942
AS-47	High-speed twin-boom bomber project with two Napier Sabres, one tractor, one pusher.	
AS-48	Projected single-seat night fighter with six 20-mm. guns. (Napier Sabre.)	
AS-49	Projected single-seat fighter/trainer to specification T.24/40. (D.H. Gipsy VI.)	
AS-50	Type number allocated to production Queen Wasps to specification T.24/40.	
AS-51	Horsa I. Troop-carrying glider to specification X.26/40	1941
AS-52	Horsa I. Bomb-carrying project to specification X.3/41	1941
AS-53	Horsa I project for vehicle transport.	
AS-54	Projected two-seater training glider to specification TX.3/43.	
AS-55	High-wing freighter project. (Two Bristol Hercules XIV, four Bristol Taurus 20, four Rolls-Royce Merlin 21, or two Bristol Centaurus.)	
AS-56	Projected single-seater fighter. (Napier Sabre VI.)	
AS-57	Ambassador. Originally projected version. (Two Bristol Hercules.)	
AS-57	Ambassador I to specification C.25/43. (Two Bristol Centaurus 631)	1947
AS-57	Ambassador I. Forty to fifty-seater production version. (Two Bristol Centaurus 661)	1950
AS-58	Horsa II. Vehicle transport with opening nose section, and twin nose wheels	1943
AS-59	Ambassador II project. (Two Bristol Proteus, two Bristol Theseus, four Napier Naiads, or four Rolls-Royce Darts.)	
AS-60	Ayrshire. Projected military transport version of Ambassador to specification C.13/45. (Two Bristol Centaurus 130.)	
AS-61	Dakota I conversion.	
AS-62	Dakota II conversion.	
AS-63	Dakota III conversion.	
AS-64	Ambassador project for R.A.F. to specification C.26/43.	
AS-65	Consul. Civil version of Oxford. (Two Armstrong Siddeley Cheetah X)	1946
AS-65	Consul Convertible and Consul Ambulance	1948
AS-66	Projected civil freighter development of Ambassador. (Two Bristol Centaurus 661.)	
AS-67	Projected civil freighter development of Ambassador. (Two Bristol Centaurus 661.)	

Glossary

A.I.D.	Aeronautical Inspection Directorate.
Aileron	Hinged sections at outboard trailing edges of wings, connected to control column to give lateral control.
Angle of attack	Angle of wing in relation to airflow.
Artificial horizon	Instrument to inform pilot of his attitude in relation to the horizon.
Booster coil	Coil to give increased spark from sparking plug.
Buffeting	Irregular oscillation of parts of an aircraft caused by the eddying wake created by other parts of it.
Cantilever wing	A wing entirely unsupported by struts or bracing wires.
Centre of gravity	Point at which aircraft will balance in the static state when loaded.
Crouch Bolas principle	The use of a number of engines distributed along the leading edge of a wing to spread the slipstream over the maximum span of the wing and give maximum lift and control at slow speeds.
Centre section	Main centre wing structure.
Desynn	An instrument in the cockpit which, by connection to a sensor attached to a control surface of the aircraft, will register the degree of movement of the surface.
Dihedral	Upward angle of wing in relation to the horizontal plane when viewed from ahead.
Directional gyro	Gyroscopically driven instrument to inform pilot of any deviation from the course he is following.
D.O.	Drawing office.
E.F.T.S.	Elementary Flying Training School.
Erk	Junior rank in R.A.F. ground staff.
Extension planes.	Sections of wing attached outboard of centre section.
Feathered (propeller)	Blades of variable pitch propeller when turned edge on to line of flight for drag reduction purposes when engine is stopped.

Flaps	Hinged panels at trailing edge of wing which can be lowered to varying angles to give increased lift and/or drag.
Flare	Action of levelling off aircraft before landing.
F.T.S.	Flying Training School.
Fuel pressure head	Pressure build-up in tank of aircraft being air-refuelled due to height of tanker above aircraft.
G.A. drawing	General arrangement drawing.
Glider	Unpowered aircraft usually unable to climb above the level of its launch point.
Gyro	Heavy flywheel, freely mounted and driven by air pressure or electricity, used to drive blind flying or auto controls.
Hydraulic ram	Piston within a cylinder, to either side of which oil can be pumped to actuate such equipment as retractable undercarriage or flaps.
Jury strut	Temporary strut.
Laminar flow wing.	Wing designed to ensure that airflow over it is consistently smooth and its path uninterrupted.
Longeron	Main structural longitudinal member in a fuselage.
Mock-up	Full scale section of a new aircraft built of normal commercial materials to prove layout of machine.
Monocoque	A type of fuselage or nacelle construction in which the main loads are taken by the skin.
Oleo leg	Shock absorbing leg of undercarriage.
O.T.U.	Operational Training Unit.
Parasol wing	Wing mounted on struts above fuselage.
Pitot head	Detector head for air pressure input to air speed indicator.
Pneumatic servo	Similar unit to hydraulic ram but utilising air pressure.
Prop turbine	Gas turbine driving propeller.
Quilting	Tendency of thin sheet metal skin to bulge within area of rivetting.
R.A.E.	Royal Aircraft Establishment.

Rib, wing or tailplane	A member which gives the required shape of the wing or tailplane and maintains that shape under load.
Rudder balance (aerodynamic)	Part of rudder surface projecting ahead of the hinge line to reduce loads on rudder bar.
Rumbold	Manufacturer of high quality aircraft seating and interior decor.
Sailplane	Superior glider capable of prolonged flight above its level of launch.
Slat	Curved section member used to guide airflow over wing.
Spar	Main structural member of a wing.
Spring tab	Adjustable control tab at trailing edge of rudder.
Stall	Airflow breakaway from wing due to insufficient relative airspeed.
Stressed skin	Skin of wing or fuselage which takes all the loads and virtually eliminates internal bracing.
Tailplane (or wing) incidence	Angle of tailplane (or wing) in relation to the datum line or fore and aft axis of the aircraft.
Townend ring cowling	Metal ring closely fitting around the cylinder heads of a radial engine.
Turn and bank indicator	Instrument to inform pilot of his rate of turn and angle of bank.
Variable pitch propeller	Propeller with blades which may be turned in flight to give most efficient angle of pitch.
Warren girder	Two beams joined by triangulated bracing.
Wing loading	Load carried per unit of area of wing.

General Index

Illustrations in bold type.

INDEX

Erratum

The illustrations on pages 106 and 114 have been transposed in error, that on page 106 being the prototype Oxford Mk.V in May, 1942, and that on page 114 being an Oxford Mk.I of the first production batch.

Index of Aircraft and Engines

Illustration and photographs in bold type.

INDEX